DOUBLE BILL

Double Bill

POEMS INSPIRED BY POPULAR CULTURE

A Sequel to *Split Screen*

Edited by Andy Jackson

RED SQUIRREL PRESS

First published in the UK in 2014 by Red Squirrel Press
www.redsquirrelpress.com

Red Squirrel Press is distributed by Central Books Ltd.
and represented by Inpress books Ltd.
www.inpressbooks.co.uk

Designed and typeset by Gerry Cambridge
gerry.cambridge@btinternet.com
Cover images by Paul Mawson

A CIP catalogue record is available from the British Library.

ISBN: 978 1 906700 95 9

Printed by Martins the Printers
www.martins-the-printers.co.uk

Editor's Introduction

In 2011, poets Tim Turnbull and Chris Emery each wrote a poem about a cult television show—Turnbull wrote about Lew Grade's stylish 60s show *The Champions* while Emery chose the US show *Mission Impossible*. The poems were aired on a Facebook conversation, one of millions of ephemeral threads of social media which flash across our screens every day. This particular thread, however, spawned an idea for a poetry project which, in turn, became the poetry anthology *Split Screen* (published by Red Squirrel Press in 2012). Poems in the anthology were inspired by TV and movies, both the popular and the obscure. The book became an event combining poetry, visuals and music with the *Split Screen* roadshow appearing at over a dozen venues and literary festivals in the two years following its publication. *Split Screen* itself became something of a cult.

In the grand tradition of the movie franchise, two years later comes the sequel; *Double Bill*, containing more poems inspired by TV and movies (and the commercials which accompany them), but this time also drawing inspiration from the worlds of music, art and sport.

Thanks go to all the poets who have supported both *Split Screen* and *Double Bill* through their poems, their appearances at roadshow events and their enthusiasm for this off-beat project. Will there be a third volume to complete an unlikely trilogy? Well, we all like a good cliff-hanger, don't we?

Andy Jackson
August 2014

For

Philip French, Dilys Powell,
Clive James & Mark Kermode

Contents

Part One

Intermission One

Part Two

Part I

Listen with Mother   Ellen Phethean

Are you sitting comfortably? Then I'll begin..
we're going to pretend that you've got some balls.

In BBC land, mother's lap
was idle, polka-dotted, placid,
safe beside a walnut wireless—

You don't know where I'm going to hide your balls—

tuned to Daphne, draped in pearls,
who played piano, telling lies
to dogs and tidy boys and girls.

Now close your eyes,
the music's going to show you where your balls are.

In my house, mother smelt of oils,
her overalls were stained with paint;
we'd come tumbling to her call.

Did you find your balls?

She'd spoonerise, play with words,
raise an eyebrow, flash a carrot,
sashay round the kitchen crooning:

Flat Foot Floozy with the floy floy.

The Colour of Hours   Joan Hewitt

Golden, that hour where it was always afternoon.
The baby upstairs, star-fished in its cot.
A single plate rinsed and shining in the rack.
The teapot warmed. And from the green transistor
ripening in sunshine on the sill, modulated
female voices conveyed a pine table of their own.

Sometimes you closed your eyes, drowsed through
Does Feminism Have a Future? and
The Best Way To Hang Your Husband's Suit,
while that sentinel of time, the ironing- board,
upright against the wall by a basket of damp shirts,
warned that the hour was never really yours.

It's not yours now in black-and-white mid- morning.
You catch a snippet in the car. Jenni Murray
trembles on a question as though it's freshly-formed
and the woman taking Botox for incontinence responds.
You switch off the engine, and the grey indefinite
of podcasts that you might download expands.

So it's a matter of parity that you want to see
a lot more penises on the small screen?...
After sixty visits, how on earth
did no-one see this child was badly injured?...
Thank you, Prime Minister. And now:
should you ever go without a bra?

On-air live from Antarctica, the Commander
of Halley Base Camp VI is used to wintering
in total darkness with twelve men; prises them
from laptops into Red Hut for a Murder game.
'And do those Saturday nights fly by?'
The Commander's giggle wings across 8,000 miles.

The Road To Wigan Casino   Daniel Cockrill

pass through arched canal path
warehouse and wharf
pit shaft and mill town
burn it down

suck in smoke choked filled
Sunday morning amphetamine fuelled
rhythm and blue hue
Seven days is too long without you

two quid in
rare disc demo spin
no moonshine no firewater no alcohol
just guts dance and Northern Soul

two tone Spencer peg clobber
twisted industrial youth truth
as you flip kick backdrop
to knees and pray

as Dean Parrish sings
I'm on my way

So it Goes…The Hacienda 1980   Carolyn Richardson

Tony, you excavated substrates of Mancunian magma
red hot seams of metal, rock
pouring through Ian's blacked out bedroom,
Sumner's bathroom cabinet
settling on a disused
Peter Street yacht showroom

Because of you the underground saw day,
anthems to a subversive, authentic new order,
writ in large in bright neon.
contrary constructivism, quirky idealism.
Loud music
anticapitalism, Mancy style.

And so it goes
undivided joy
strong drink, drugs in the toilets, mad highs
blue Mondays on the come down.

I was there in the sharp jagged noise,
in the hot press of jumping bodies
head spinning from excess.
Fairground ride tube lighting
the rush of cold air in the car park
Lindsay in a van, pants by her ankles
You largeing it with Pete in the bar.

And so it went
Curtis dead—bands filched by Morley, London
ZTT records, Trevor Horn calling the tune
apartments now on the dark side of Whitworth Street
At night canal streets quiet as the grave.
Tony underground.

Biography   Jon Stone

Cloughie is keen.
Cloughie is without doubt.
Cloughie is deserving.

Cloughie is a 19-year-old guy.
Cloughie is an unknown quantity.
Cloughie is sending out his signal.

Cloughie is unveiled.
Cloughie is on his way.
Cloughie is sparking up.
Cloughie is in charge.
Cloughie is brutal.
Cloughie is set.

Cloughie is running.
Cloughie is a ram.
Cloughie is the prime example.
Cloughie is ours.
Cloughie is theirs.
Cloughie is a shrewd operator.
Cloughie is a common thread.

Cloughie is spinning.
Cloughie is in a state.
Cloughie is solipsistic, paranoid.
Cloughie is done.
Cloughie is offline.
Cloughie is legend.
Cloughie is a bloody legend.
Cloughie! Is that you?

Frankly, Mr Shankly   Eddie Gibbons
i.m. Peter Gilmore

Your rosette might have painted the first splash of blue
on the Anfield gates that Saturday the news from
Sheffield threatened to crush the spirit of Shankly.
You might even have been there, the Henry Winter
of your era, sharing Press Box disbelief to hear the final
whistle blow before anyone had time to catch their breath.

Adoring both the Gwladys and the Kemlyn, football
was a double bill for you: Saturdays about you were
either end of Stanley park, entranced by Golden Visions
and Anfield Irons alike. Scrawling match reports
in the mist of smoke and breathings on bus windows,
you were grooming for a life soaked in printer's ink.

During lessons you were mentally interviewing Bill:
Frankly, Mr. Shankly, will the position held by Morrissey
ever be filled by that charming man named Smith?

You alone in school knew the meaning of *Nil Satis*
Nisi Optimum, the origin of the tower on the crest,
and which of Mother Nobletts and Old Ma Bushell
won the toffee lady franchise wars. You were gone
before some Kop wag gave a handbag to Gordon West:
gone before we sang *Careless Hands* to Gary Sprake.

A father bent and muted by the Hirohito camps, a mother
whose eyes could not lift higher than her prayer-gloved
hands, read the only headline to have your name below it.
A wreath of red, a wreath of blue, Aretha sang *For All*
We Know and left your parents pondering those things
that football's more important than.

The Ghost Train—a Twinned Sonnet   John Glenday

Roy, this is how it finishes: we're riding Dante's Inferno
    together—
that cheapskate ghost train where Fred Hale hides from his
    killers
in Brighton Rock. I'm Fred, of course, and you're my friendly
    murderer,
my twin, the one doomed to be sitting alone when the car
    shudders

to a halt in the din and glare of a South Coast early summer.
This is what life is all about—cheap shocks and clapboard
    horrors
the whole scene clichéd and overblown—the way the two of
    us peer
down into the abyss beneath the rails: a seethe of black,
    impatient water

fretting the stanchions that hold us clear of purgatorial fire.
When you looked into my face, you looked into a mirror,
and smiled, and took my shoulder, held me safe, then pushed
    me over.
My eyes opened five minutes early, yours closed two decades
    late.

Is that the tide I hear behind us, or the ghost-train's plywood
    thunder,
or the clutter clutter clutter of loose film clearing the gate?
John, you died two decades early, I was born five minutes late.
Two frames of the one short film—that's really all we were.

Now that one frame is cut, I'll carry back twice the weight—
your life folded in mine—to 1921. We're boys again—back in the
    foyer

of the Regent with Nanny. Valentino breaks her dusty heart four
times in a single week. We saw it here for the first time—the
    raw power

of film: that dance! Death galloping from the clouds, the Great
    War
breaking like a sea against their lives, and in the end, *The End*,
    a blur
of shadows between fresh graves, the audience all shiftless
    whispers.
A hundred times we sat in that immense, small dark, and
    breathed air

rich with smoke and sweat—the reek of a strange, new fire.
    Remember,
we filed out glazed and dumb with joy and dark—back to the
    trashy glare
of life going dimly on. John, next time we stumble out into the
    light together,
guess which of us will blink, and which will disappear?

COEN BROTHERS

Coenesque: flare to white/fade in from white Pippa Little

In another life did I come to Fargo?
Me, Joel and Ethan Coen in a back seat rental hire
past the endless fence, the film-noir snow,
Siberia with family restaurants where I set my hair on fire.

Between Joel and Ethan Coen in a Cutlass Ciera hire
I searched for that other life, the one true story,
Siberia with family restaurants, where I set my hair on fire,
The Jolly Troll Tavern in its treacly neon glory.

I searched for that other life, my one true story,
Marge Gunderson my mother, O Brothers Where Art Thou?
The Jolly Troll Tavern in its treacly neon glory,
One righteous road to go as far as fate will allow:

Marge Gunderson my mother, O Brothers Where Art Thou?
We could have been happy here, this I surely know!
One righteous road to go as far as fate will allow—
in another lifetime I'll find you all in Fargo.

Old Blue Eyes   George Szirtes

Old Blue Eyes, the distinct upbeat strut
of your brassy tenor takes me back to a land
of my fathers that never quite was. The band
strikes up, the door swings open and shut
on you, cool dude, in your depression gear,
your box of blades, your rat pack in its cage.
Hoboken bruiser of my father's age,
we're in the bar at the back end of the year,
it's quarter to three, and it's your voice that rings
in the notional juke-box. The war is over.
From here to eternity means this is for ever.
The drunks howl how it was just one of those things,
another for the road. The icy blue eyes
are closing. The mob prepares its cold replies.

Things We Can't Untie Jacqueline Saphra

My boyfriend crashed the week before the concert
I'd been waiting for, as if he'd planned to miss it.
I took out Songs of Leonard Cohen, let the record
spin through silence, wiped it clean and put the stylus
where I wanted it, that smooth place in between
the grooves, and waited till it stuck: *I'm not looking*
for another I'm not looking for another I'm not looking
for another I'm not looking for another I'm not looking
for another. I sold my boyfriend's ticket to a girl
with hunger I could recognise, fought to the front
so Leonard knew my longings, gave me all his songs,
took my tears in return. Later, he signed his name
across my chest and sang *Oh come with me my little one,*
and when he touched my eyes, *our kisses deep*
and warm, and said *We are so small between the stars,*
so large against the sky, I couldn't feel my boyfriend
any more: the leaning green of his Mohican or
The Guns of Brixton lurching through his boom box
that night he took the key of his Triumph Tiger,
scratched it loud across Songs of Leonard Cohen, left me
with a broken record, just because I wouldn't ride
behind him, didn't like to go that fast, because I said
I didn't trust the brakes.

Prince Buster   Nancy Somerville

I don't remember being taught at school
anything of Glasgow's guilty past,
why the streets that led to the Clyde
were Jamaica, Virginia, Glassford,
or how the ships brought bloodied wealth
and mansions built for tobacco lords
in the second city of Empire.

Then, in the sixties,
the trade winds blew in
Cecil Bustamente Campbell.
We were east-end teenagers
spinning his *Blue Beat*
in after-school bedrooms,
dancing in dark weekend clubs
to music like we'd never heard
—wailing sirens, screeching car brakes
and that scratchy, Caribbean voice,
chkta chkta chkta chkta
hot, dangerous, exotic.
Don't call him *Scarface*, he's so cool
he's *Freezing Up Orange Street*
and his soul is Ska,
the original *Judge Dread* passing sentence
on gangsters and rude boys.

From *Ghost Dance* to *Ghost Town*
and beyond, the music's heart
beats on
while the citadels of the barons remain.

O{+>   Charlie Jordan

I wasn't ready.
Just 14, a six foot girl, the classroom nerd
when I first heard your dirty funk,
but not with my ears.
Innocent regions responded
not knowing why.

Liquorice-lined peacock eyes
seduced me into puberty.
Purple-exed by Liberace lace,
high heeled boots, raw Hendrix beats.
Patti Smith's antithesis.

And you loved women.
Honoured their potency,
from Sheila E, to Sheena E.
What if I was your girlfriend?
I tried to climb inside your lyrics—
love letters from Alphabet Street.
What would you do with my Cherry Moon?

I joined your revolution,
guillotined Grandad's trilby,
threaded home-permed hair
tumbling over my left eye like ivy from a hanging basket
and pressed Play.
Paisley Power armoured me
against hostile school bus stares.
They weren't ready.

You quivered my concrete city.
Within each realm of purple reign
you remain beyond reach.
Delicious questions, but some enigmas need no answers.
Thirty years on,
I'm nearly ready for you.

Loose Fit   Alan Smithee

We formed the band a day before the NME
came north to give a nameless scene a name,
impose the new aesthetic, set agendas. We
slept on buses back to sink estates, shamed

by narrowness of trouser, perfected our hair,
waited for the man. The man never showed.
Some white trash went overground, where
major labels rushed to mine the mother lode

for breaks and basslines which the legal teams
would clear. The rest of us tuned up in dance
halls, played to high-rise groupies, schemed
in chippy queues how we'd blow the advance.

Our older brothers spoke of how it used to be
in '76, when everyone unlearnt the chords,
played it fast and hard, little caring for the key,
and something happened when you hit *record*,

but back in '89 the boys I knew were mad for it,
or just plain mad, but always looking to score.
Some of this is just the way it was, or a loose fit,
but my god, Madchester, so much to answer for.

there's something sad Andrew McMillan

there's something sad
about the curled book
at the bottom of the box
looking like the man in the bar
who people forget they used to want to talk to

like the boy with the glass lips   the unclean
hair that smells of wine   who quietly contains
a secret nobody will miss   except

weeks from now   when you suddenly wonder
where he is   what it was he used to say   the way
sitting on a bus   you wonder what happened
to the bus conductors   after they were torn out of the city

DAVID HOCKNEY

Mr and Mrs Clark and Percy Alan Buckley
1970–71, acrylic paint on canvas

I like the way you capture that chic milieu—
Ossie's chrome-frame chair, the white telephone
casually untabled on the carpet, Celia's
purple smock dress. And I like how I'm shown
too much, the genre subverted: husband seated,
not wife; no flow of gaze from one to the other
to viewer, but both facing me from either
side of the window's gulf. I'm made complicit,
a triangle's third point. But what I love is the cat,
Blanche given Percy's name; you decided that
was artistically correct. Back turned to me it sits,
slender and erect, on Ossie's faithless lap,
staring out at something beyond all this
deceit, at something beyond my grasp.

DAMIEN HIRST

Shark Tale   George Szirtes

1

It was, as we know, the shark
Looming out of the dark,
An abortion from the ark,
With which he made his mark,

A pickled hunk of fear
Grinning from ear to ear,
So vast, so still, so near:
The Great Idea flung clear.

A fortune needs just one.
The pickled cow begun
After the shark was done
Was simply carrying on

The notion as discovered.
As for the rest: plain buggered.

2.

The shark enters the brain
And squats there like the night.
You won't go there again.
You know it isn't right.

The ancient fairy tale
As sold to you online.
The market that can't fail
Done to the old design.

Ah, Damien, the pitch
Remains just as it was.
The cows are breaking rich.
The dying flies still buzz.

There's nowhere left to hide.
Here's the formaldehyde.

Daft As A Brush   Andy Jackson

Hollow-eyed and grunting, infested
by the scent of death and embrocation,
he works the civic centres, expected
to accept each win as consolation

for years in damp gymnasia. Matted golden
hair, porcine belly, blood-stained trunks,
mask genius escapes from pins and holds,
inhuman shrugging-off of body checks.

No close-ups as his head is lowered, dashed
by forearm blows to which he has no answer,
till the grey-fleshed wraith of pain, smashed
in his daze, leaps up like some fell dancer

roughhousing under crushing argon lights.
The baying crowd close in around the ring,
urge him to the turning of the fight,
sense the move that moves without him.

Then it comes, and every head is turned
to him. Les's leather jowls are shaken,
fog of sweat descends. Muscles burn,
the canvas dips and, in a blur, my life is taken.

Split Decision   Hilda Sheehan

Before his nose was broken
she knew nothin
about boxin: no smokin

no drinkin no foolin around durin
trainin—women weaken
legs. To her it was Thanksgivin

(a turkey in the oven)
just a Thursday to him, 'Come on in—
some soda, some donuts or somethin?

Meet Cuff and Link. YO! how you doin?'
'What's the attraction?' Adrian
without glasses was stunnin

in her cute red hat there waitin, breakin
hearts. 'Don't you leave town, Adrian!'
Ding! Ding! three, five, and seven

to fifteen rounds of fightin
the Italian Stallion
spat nails, ate lightnin.

'What were you thinkin
on the fifteenth?' WHAT? ADRIAN!
'Ladies and gentlemen your attention

please.' ROCKY! ADRIAN!
ROCKY! ROCKY! ROCKY! ADRIAN!
'We have a split decision!'

ROCKY! ROCKY!—ADRIAN! *I love YOU*, ADRIAN!

10 Cento, or *'Conversation in my Father's Car, Pearl Jam on Shuffle'*   Mark Burnhope

Began as Mookie Blaylock (basketballer). O dear
Dad, can you see me now? Their demos then
became *Ten*. Something to echo in my un-
known future's ear: finally the shades are raised.
(Red) Hot Sound (Garden) Jam, Temple
of the Dog—heaven knows
if there's a ceiling, I don't want to be held
in your debt. This broken
wheel is coming undone—shit, so much it
don't show. Byzantine reflected
in our pond; three crooked hearts, swirls
all around. The drummers debate: of the
infamous PJ three which is your favourite
                (Dave A., Jack, Matt) and why
                        was Dave fired? A wave came
crashing like a fist to the jaw, delivered him
wings. What I know is Ed detested Dave's
(glorified) adherence to guns. Like
                he's riding
                        on a motorbike
                in the strongest wind.
'Return to form' progress laced with ram-
ifications. We all walk the long road, lost
nine friends we'll never know (Roskilde Festival stage
collapsed). Ransom paid the devil. Model, role
model, roll some models (Neil Young, The Who,
Ramones, Pink Floyd) in blood. Loss of agency!
Why let the sad song play? Lifetimes are
catching up with me. We're here, Seattle—
see that Needle? More than
friends, I always pledged: I will walk with my hands
bound. My glasses, the glove-box, would you mind?

Be Bold, Be Bold, But Not Too Bold   Elizabeth Rimmer

I thought Teen Spirit smelled of Lynx,
discarded apples from your lunch-box,
wet trainers, crisps, the heavy metal sweat
of boy. And then I heard that Muddy Waters
song: '*My girl, my girl, don't you lie to me,
tell me where did you sleep last night.*'
My inappropriate high voice and folk style
made you laugh. I taught you chords
to *Come as You Are.* You joined a band,
and when they ditched you, the hurt
was worse than when girls dumped you
texting from new mobile phones.
Now I'm listening again, more carefully.
All Apologies. Lithium. About A Son.
That bluebeard voice raw, savage, beautiful,
unlocks the secret room that sullen
adolescent silences concealed.
It's full of butchered teenage hopes.
Your life is good now, and we talk often,
but still I can't unknow.
*What else should I write?
I don't have the right.
I shiver the whole night through.*

You can't get the wood, you know Colin Will

They called me Nadger, a schoolboy/Boy Scout nickname
that lasted a year, maybe two, from 'The Great Nadger Plague'.
We had catchphrase conversations after every broadcast,
and attempted to mimic all the voices
when ours had only just broken. I could do Eccles,
another friend was Bluebottle (strikes heroic pose),
Moriarty and the Major were up for grabs
and we competed for authentic-type raspberries.
A suave-sounding boy was Hercules Grytpype-Thynne
for a term, but was dropped when no longer funny.
One buddy did all the characters, was Minnie Bannister
to my Henry Crun, later worked in broadcasting.
Bluebottle took up bass guitar, went into business, did well.
The Famous Eccles was a drop-out, then a poet.
Nobody wanted to be Neddie Seagoon: too straight,
a short, fat fool, a silly, twisted boy—not like us.
We did without the Max Geldray and Ray Ellington breaks,
too young to go round the corner for the old brandy.

After the last exam came the diaspora of adulthood.
Some have fallen in the water, a couple are deaded.
I don't have the urge to remake old programmes,
won't renew friendships based on words
of lost times nicked from a better script writer.

'Shut up Eccles.'
'Yersh, shut up Eccles.'

Small Steps   A F Harrold

It was Orwell, remember, who charmingly observed
that the sillier the walk, the graver the situation—
the harder the grope back to daylight is going to be.

Do this, like this—no, like this!

The goose-step could never catch on in England, he said.
Our embarrassment being good guard against Fascism:
the inoculating image of Cleese entering the Ministry.

Growing Up With The X-Men   Adam Horovitz

Before lycra became metaphor
for skin, and hormones rose in rebellion
against innocence, before grief
unwound itself into tempered adulthood,

I lived for the pixelated primary colours
splashed monthly on pulp paper, the giddy fix
of teenagers who fought like gods in gaudy,
skintight cloth, who clung to dreams of survival
as if they were a slipping mask.

It was love by recognition; I was
the sad circus devil in blue fur,
the new mutant who'd lost his mother,
the cast-off, the reject, dreaming he ran reckless, willing

out to fight dark-but-brightly-clad reflections of himself:
eyes spurting fire; calling down the sky
to his songs of power; vanishing and appearing
in puffs of acrid smoke. A marvel of mutation
who slipped past sorrow and was reborn.

That thrill is muted now by measured griefs:
the late-paid monthly bill; the yellowing hopes of love.
Except, sometimes, when the moon slips closer down the hill
or too much wine's been drunk,

I see my mother unashing like a Phoenix
out of loose-inked sketches of the past
whilst nightcrawlers and shadowcats
phase and fight and Bamf their way, rejoicing,
                          to the edge of dream.

Caught in The DC Multiverse   Bob Beagrie

It wasn't the lack of comedy that led me to detect
that all was not as it seemed in the world of captions,
speech bubbles, those block printed sound effects
as I slipped between the irregular frames of each
graphically inked instant of dramatic action where no
one ever watched the garden while sipping a glass
of lemonade without it being laced with deadly poison
or gamma radiation or without the peaceful summer
scene being shattered by the imminent invasion of a
psychopathic alien in a skin-tight costume of primary
colours whose destiny was to consume all worlds
and the lemonade drinking garden-watcher was none
other than our all-time favourite cosmic, battle
seasoned saviour cunningly disguised as common
or garden Joe Shmo to lure the planet devouring
super-villain into a false sense of security, to land him
Slap-Bang in the trap of advanced science from which,
eventually, he'll manage to escape and flee, tail tucked
between his legs, but vowing revenge and promising
to return by issue #156; leaving me to misinterpret
every mundane occurrence as the lead in to some
apocalyptic struggle between Good and Evil, all for
the sake of a scarred soul but held secure behind
its vigilante mask of justice and self-sacrifice; while
sitting on the corrugated garage roof we'd talk in half
worried tones about all those big questions like how
many sit ups it would take to build a six pack like
Superman's, how practical was the length of Batman's
cape and what in the multiverse were we supposed
to do to start growing pubic hair, down there.

Into the Desert With No Name   Ryan Van Winkle

The end of the world is a desert.
I am in no hurry. I live where I can

broadcast before you, faithful dog
of my youth. Sing along when I can

with tea, lady fingers, Quaker Oats.
I have a stock set of sweating dreams:

going onstage & forgetting lyrics, still
find myself naked on a busy street, at school

unprepared for the final exam, falling
off a cliff, turning Radar Love up loud

on the M8, drumming the wheel to feel
my brakes won't brake. Like dreams

the music kids blast gets stranger. Once
I scratched *Ladies and gentlemen,*

please comply. Shit not on the seat
but straight in the eye! It was ink

and electric. My private, toilet history
ridiculous even humiliating. I keep singing

my own story. My daughter has eyes
rolling like silver dials. They'll stop spinning

and she'll tune in to the station that tells
her own life in the inarticulate air. A dead sparrow

hanging from a Morrissey tree, a mark dancing
on my ceiling, the shape of an arrow.

A Phil Collins song, signs, you know,
we need them more than dreams. For the cross

roads. For the high desert noon, pointing
like a faithful dog who remembers

where we've been
when we cannot.

Radio 4   Luke Kennard

I love how you create what you report
I said on AM, then by PM heard
He loves how we create what we report.

I don't know how the prizes were conferred,
too complicated for an argument;
a gentleman's *omerta* is preferred

to chinks of light between prepared statements—
you taste for imperfections not for fun—
you catch them in a lie, you pitch your tents

again a little further from the sun.
The science of carbon dating, peak oil, Khartoum…
It's probably the same for everyone.

Without you all the kitchens feel like tombs—
You give some context to the washing up;
You make a university of rooms.

An Invitation to the Dance Tim Turnbull

On railway journeys or in meetings—
deluged by the waves of tedium
that are the strongly-held opinions,
liberally and volubly declaimed,
of strangers; or collegial bleatings,
inscrutable without a medium
or simultaneous translation,
so enigmatic, so arcane
their communicators' systems seem
attuned to different frequencies—
does your reverie increase to trance?
Your body throb and muscles twitch?
Does your every living fibre scream
for jazz-ballet dream sequences?
Kick over the boardroom table; dance
into a carriage aisle from which
the drear quotidian ebbs away
revealing the bright Minnellian
hues of the outer spheres: the air
crackles with the startled blare of horns;
a syncopated, wild array
musters, set upon rebellion
against the workaday; and see there,
from out of the aether comes, borne
on zephyrs, sporting wingèd pumps,
the messenger, firm thighed, athletic,
fit as a fiddle, and attended
by fey gangsters who click and jerk
jazz-handed. As he spins and jumps,
submit to this blithe hermetic
prince, and feel your reality blended
into his camp *Gesamtkunstwerk.*

Fred   Isobel Dixon

*'Fred Astaire and Ginger Rogers were sexy, but only
with their feet, like butterflies.'*—Clive James

Forget dancing backwards in high heels and all that jazz—
I've told you before, I want to be *Fred*.

A sparrow of a chap turned shining blackbird,
magpie-tuxed, woodpecker heel-

and-toe, but gliding swallow-tailed, smooth
as you please. Mr Anti-Gravity. Impossible

geometries of flair and speed. No map.
I ache for the ease, the froth of her skirt,

the gloss of his shoes. And yet am sick
of so much breeziness, balsawood plots,

paper plane trajectories. She can fluff those ostrich
feathers up all she likes, if he's in love

with anything it's the *steps*. Sometimes
in a solo, there's a glint, a glimpse—of what?

All of this perfect lightness.
Where on earth did you find it, Mr Austerlitz?

The Grecian Urn Sally Evans

They danced for real for two decades and more
on high-speed unforgiving ice. We saw

their flawless synchrony over spacious floors.
Audiences raved. They took perfect scores.

They swooped and spun, came together and fled,
body understanding body, legs steady,

a consummate illusion of easy play.
Even the hard woman prime minister of the day

declared that she would like to see them wed.
They sought deliberate worlds apart, pledged

as they were to perfection. Today, ageing, they sit
together and say, of course we dabbled in it,

courtship. We showed our stamina, were tough,
and dancing together was enough.

Stay young on their behalf, computer, screen the videos,
each year, story, steps, music and clothes,

image for all the truth of beauty as they turn
forever fair, forever searching, round their Grecian Urn.

Pearl & Dean   Hazel Buchan Cameron

Reeled in with an instant ident
We're taken elsewhere in time
before the blockbuster begins.
And stars are no match
for the asteroids that flare—
so briefly, and warn
of a doomed planet in flames…

We look on unaware
it will be music
pa pa pa pa pa
that resonates beyond all image,
to carry the heat of us
and grief of us
long after the final—DAH

Watch With Mother   Julie Boden

I've said it once, I'm telling you again
they're not all Daddy Woodentops you know.
Take care, she said. Beware when dating men

—a rag and bobtail bunch, she said, so when
a good one comes along…don't let him go!
I've said it once. I'm telling you again.

If we marked all these jokers out of ten
the ones who come to play—they'd be *zero*.
Take care, she said. Beware, when dating men.

Some love a drink and these two, Bill and Ben,
they need a Little Weed to face each show
I've said it once; I'm telling you again.

The gardener? Ah, he veers towards a *ten*.
He works. He sweats. He'll make your garden grow.
Take care, she said. Beware when dating men.

I've met all sorts. I had to learn the zen
of dating, darling…blow by painful blow.
I've said it once, I'm telling you again.
Take care, she said. Beware…when dating men.

Mice and the Broken Sky   Helen Ivory

And when the night sky shattered into pieces
she gathered them all up to take to Bagpuss
intrigued to know exactly what he'd think
and how the mice would set about their sewing
and patching of the moon to make a story
sound enough to drape in the shop window,

so anybody walking past the window
might recognise their own sky from the pieces
and trace the hieroglyphics of their story
all rearranged and then recast by Bagpuss;
mouse blood in the moon from frantic sewing
because it's hard to think a thing and then unthink.

The requirement of mouse is not to think
but make things clean and shiny for the window
yet sometimes their hearts bleed into their sewing
and sometimes their own skies break into pieces.
All eyes and ears are firmly fixed on Bagpuss,
that he might think them all a better story.

The owner of the sky might like a story
where they're a mouse and never have to think.
They'll hand their bills and keys over to Bagpuss,
spend singing days just focussed on the window
whose sky is whole and not made up of pieces,
where days are held in place by careful sewing.

The duty of a mouse is in the sewing;
and underpinning logic to each story
which clearly is made up of broken pieces.
The requirement of a mouse is not to think,
but visualise the sky held by the window.
Sometimes they fancy they invented Bagpuss.

In the tale where they invented Bagpuss
they buckled down all night together, sewing.
And next day from thin air, they made a window
then dipped their tails in ink to write the story
of a cloth cat who was bold enough to think
he could fabricate a perfect sky from pieces.

Pick up your pieces; let's commence the sewing!
Bagpuss has donned his thinking cap to think.
So let your story breathe; shatter the window!

Outnumbered   Heather Reid

You thought there'd be a script, some guidance notes,
and not this *laissez faire* approach
where all the dialogue is improvised,
and you're supporting actor to the kids.
Some days you wonder if it's real;
each episode seems endless and
increasingly the humour's hard to find
in glib one- liners, off-the-cuff.
Until, at last, the closing scene:
a story read, a ruffled head, then
up the hill to Bedfordshire, lights out,
goodnight, I love you;
a look, caught by the camera,
as you bend to kiss your wife,
how's that for acting?

The Addams Family   Sheila Templeton

Sic gorgiamus allos subjectatos nunc

Ah Gomez—and Morticia
you never knew why I hung about
that summer—spent long afternoons
in the swamp behind 1001 Cemetery Lane
—helped Uncle Fester detonate his caps
(and stuck his toupee back on straight)
sharpened Pugsley's guillotine—daily
so Wednesday's doll could swoon, forever headless
—defied death from strangulation feeding Cleopatra,
your favourite African Strangler plant
—I see them still—those chunks of raw meat—dripping.
Evenings you watched me practise dance with Lurch
the *watusi*, the *hully-gully*—and yes, I'll not deny
that granite face and thick lipped leer—a big turn on.
And his voice. That voice. *Neat. Sweet. Petite.*
I brushed up your French, so you could thrill Gomez
all over again, your little *bubbale*. Remember
how your pronunciation of *merveilleux* cured
his bronchitis, that first time? You'd barely met.
And oh—your *cool*—Morticia. That skin tight black
became you like a moon-starved night, all hobble skirted
octopus tendrils waving in delicious invitation,
slaughtering roses to make bouquets of thorns,
boiling up his favourite crunchies, eye of newt and cold yak
—for Gomez, your horny crazy kohl-eyed husband filling
his plus fours with such panache—don't get me wrong—
it was never a trial, never an endurance. Who wouldn't enjoy?
But that wasn't *why*. The truth is—I was in love,
head over heels, beyond explanation, beyond reason
in love with—*Thing*. That sinewy, bony, paler than pale
sexy, disembodied hand, opening his box wherever needed
scratching your back, handing tissues, tea, massage—
I *wanted* him, the way he beckoned, the way
he crooked that long forefinger...

Quickener   Ira Lightman

Sharp bold suits and parting'd cuts *BOB*
legs a trellis of moving scissors *BOB*
Sir has many knees *BOB*

Never did grand phrasery
so balloon the chops and eyeballs *BOB*
You papier mache elephant man *flash* *BOB*

You between of punk and new romantic *BOB*
the colours *BOB* in an easy wearing lasting
fabric *BOB* Big broad face and forehead

of Jim Reeves *BOB* and I'd say Victor
Mature from Viz *BOB* not Vic Ramone *BOB*
though you now say of neither

whose dad and grandad share
the name Jim Moir *BOB* and birthday
with you *BOB* How wouldn't you surrealize the norm?

And now I'm in the North *BOB* And you live
where I grew up *BOB* in Kent *BOB* or did *BOB* I was a fan
before your skit of Aldington on Sea *BOB*

Jim Moir to Vic Reeves: more jocular *BOB*
vim in the roar *BOB* a gem me *BOB* Intelligence
and art practice in your fooling *BOB*

and each next frame like a new track on an album *BOB*
all gesture and pause and bang *BOB* Smuttily forward
and this is never me *BOB*

The Church of Bartholomew And Wiseman   Kevin Cadwallender

And this is just a repeat, a repeat in the schedules
A repeat of a poem what I wrote, of men merging into myth
Of two men in pyjamas, sharing the duvet of our memories.
And what would it take for a kiss?
Chloroform… and what would it take for this?
A short, fat, hairy poem where you cannot see the join
Or the object landing in the brown paper bag
For another 4 pound you could have had Seamus Heaney
And as my Dad was so fond of repeating
at the drop of an ambulance,
He won't sell much ice cream at that speed
And Angela Rippon having legs
and Shirley Bassey having boots
And what do you think of it so far?

And this poem is about a yard short
of laughter shared between me and my Father.
Repeats in the back issues of the Radio Times
From the brand new bright yesterdays
Of the church of Morecambe & Wise;
Our Eric and Ernie who art in heaven
Hallowed be thy names.
And this is just Arthur Tolcher
Sneaking in as the credits roll,
Look at me when I'm talking to you.
And this is just me saying
All the right words, all the right words
But not necessarily in the right order
I'll give you that, I'll give you that sunshine.

Nina Speaks★   Naomi Woddis

Every day is a matter
of survival.
I had to freeze my soul
in ice, sacrifice
my whole life
to music.

Music is my God.
When the show starts
keep your eyes on me
and don't worry about nothing.

I want you to get it right—
I am Doctor Nina Simone, music is my God.
Every day is a matter of survival.

★*Everything in this poem was, at some point, said by
Nina Simone herself*

The Black Tapestry of Amy Winehouse   Janette Ayachi

Ancestry tarot-marked by Jazz, upholstered with narcotics
   as she evolved
past the spinning-wheel when managers tried to customize her
   patchwork—
no rehab for the dolls made from the rags of gold Queens
   and the glory of small Gods.

She scaled billboard music charts the way hot mercury
   shoots up glass
one million copies sold in one esoteric summer of weight loss
   and mood swings.
A rag doll with buttons for eyes, four holes taproots to the fabric
   veins of her soul,
her stitched-on mouth gaping an alembic tunnel of deep
   contralto.

Just a Jewish girl singing along to old records in her lost room,
hyperthermia under the sheets, Librium and fame just wasn't
   enough to save her
from the police arrests, needle-point coma and the curse of
   irregular heartbeats.

That morning in July her bodyguard found her in bed
   cotton stuffing spilled from limbs,
scraps of notations and empty vodka bottles,
   her sewed on smile the only thing intact.

Lips blue like willow-pattern bone china, dipped in purple haze,
   her voodoo twin
up late mixing potions into an almanac of addictions, a spinneret
   of stark ritual, elbow-deep
in candle-light and relic, self-harm scars sutured across corners,
   moon-slit at the seams.

Pulse-snagged, lungs unzipped, heart ink-poisoned
   by a toxic red felt tip,

as flammable as petrol, cremated to tribute as prayers emitted
    from floods of fan mail
and the basic grammar of conjugated stars spoofed
    into tabloid personas.

Now angels as giddy as schoolgirls hover around her head like
    bees
weaving braids into her hive of wool, sharing the pillow with her
    dreams.
'I'm not ashamed but the guilt will kill me if you jump first'.

Unbound   Lindsey Holland

It's possible, if improbable, that you are not
a single being, shifting from lab to studio,

bulrush to kelp, but are instead a wave of yourself,
the cells of which arrive not on a point nor in the line

of a human figure, but splattered through space. Given this,
I can't predict where you'll be, though when I look

you're there, star-toothed, your cheekbones ripened
to a lacquer in the flash of camera photons, or otherwise

meandering through data streams, your binary read
and assembled into lips, the charcoal of your T-shirt,

galactic-glosses of fringe, and the push and pull
of broad words, tongue taps. You always will appear

but only because I expect it. When I turn away
you're anywhere: a breath of hyperactive follicles

and mouthfuls of moon. There are planets inside you
which fit within sugar cubes and crumble, cascade

into states of higher entropy. I think of you asleep
in vacuum, tumbled, or coasting through a twist of holes,

a speck in flesh unbound, like me, an unskeletal
decillion times yourself, and nothing particular.

Me, Brian Cox (the other one)   Chrissy Williams

I was the voice of God.
Take that, atheism. I
generally play villains,
so this was a change
of pace. God spoke
sonorously and in Scots.
Who knew? You, deep down,
like a twitch in Sunday thighs:
God sounds like you.

But it's not enough.
I'll paint my house blue,
blue the colour of sky,
blue the colour of God's home.
So when the devil calls for sinners,
he'll see God's blue and pass me by.
I need the false idol reassurance.
I need a blanket of blue paint
because, although my sins
are not all grievous,
they are not few.

The Counterplayer Gazes In and Lives to Play the Tale   Dzifa Benson

1. On the cliff face of this wet indigo, he is the man who tied water.

2. A trumpet sounds: the prince is in a hurry to dance on the street.

3. Sometimes it sounds like the boom of the earth stretching and yawning. Sometimes it's as erudite as a tabla. Most times it's as if he's about to regurgitate a star.

4. When I die
Turn no corner
Bend no curve
Take me straight to Agorko

5. What kind of food is a song?

6. He'll see you in that space between finger and pluck, between the decay of sound and the priest who tells you these palm oil plantations have been a 1000 years in the making.

7. With spoilt embouchure I carry a sputtering flame in this house of mirrors, rip the mother of all sorrows into the sky.

8. He spits stories of the Mami Wata, coils of serpents around her neck.

9. I'll tell you of Iroko and baobab, of a bracelet made of an elephant's tusk, of cotton in my ears and blood gurgling in my throat.

10. What is the meaning of a red baritone sax on the five spot?

11. Kokuvi has covered his eyes with his hands and is using his jaw to see.

The Boys in the Corner Won't be Told   Tim Wells

Wrapped tight,
change in yer pocket rattlin',
beer in hand so cold.
Sounds and pressure.

Tough bass…killin' the place,
an' every man off'a 'im face.
Zinc fence dances, blues,
sweaty cellar clubs,

head rockin', shoulders swayin',
feet doin' a likkle likkle shuffle.
Clock the jacket, flash the linin',
'It's gonna be rougher yet.'

Sweat starts to roll
and the night drops its pace:
checking sorts but steppin', steppin',
steppin' on.

The weight of the world
ain't as heavy as the bass,
the gap between what we have
and for what we strive

opens, that moment of static
as the DJ picks up the mic'
and the next cut drops.

Saint Laurent   Max Wallis

Where did we first say the word?
I know it was somewhere inert,

unimportant. No bed, no spread of skin,
just a battery of lights, a hive of flashes.

I remember your antiqued face,
those bruised eyes,

the thin bones of your birdbeak mask,
that mop fringe: a visor to peer under.

How many times did we say it after?
How many times did we mean it?

Ben Sherman or *What are you doing wanting a lad's shirt anyway?*   Joan Johnston

Deep-pink cotton. Button-down collar. Loop at the back.
Pleat. In an attempt to straighten my pan-caked face
she's bought me a fake from C&A's
and I'll never get away with it, how will I get away
tonight, sneak out in my threadbare-but-at-least-it's-credible
Brutus Trim-Fit instead? She'll be checking
at the door *So come on, let's see it then*
and she is. *Honestly, it looks lovely pet
and no-one will ever know the difference.
69/11d just for a shirt! Ben who?*

Oh, that youth club dance I never went into. Bottled it
—had no choice. Said goodbye to any chance with Trev or Dave
or Mod Tom (gorgeous, I heard, in a brand new yellow one),
had to keep my three-quarter length maroon leather coat on
and hang about clock-watching all night in the church porch
with Existential Pete from the Upper 6th
—horn-rimmed glasses and a bulky jumper, a practising
Outsider, though to his credit he really was
inhaling all those Players Number 6—
who quoted me Camus in the original French, at some length,
before resorting to a pompous, posh Geordie:
History is made, Joan, and never bought
then lapsing, finally, into the desperate authentic
—something about the importance of *ploughing wor own furrows
    so how about it?*

Ferryman   Tiffany Atkinson

Call that a fucking coin—you couldn't punt
a rubber whore with that. Wrong boat? Oh really?
Hop the fuck in, pal, or fuck the fuck off. See you,
that can no more unshackle yersel from the slack-
wanking choob of the flesh than the last cunt?
Yes, you're dead, and yes, I am not a nice man,
and here's the triple whammy: this dark's
longer, thicker, harder than a navvy
after thirteen years at sea, and down
its bitter end there's just a wee brat
mewling for his mammy. That's what you get
son, that's what you get. So all aboard
the Skylark! Don't ask me, you finger of piss:
no fucker knows what happens after this.

Mary Whitehouse demonstrates Newton's 3rd law of motion   Nikki Robson

We women of Britain object
    Clean Up TV!
            Cat's eye lenses magnify
            a slide into sex
            at tea time. Lips form a pout
            against open-mouthed kisses,
            pen poised between the sheets.

to the propaganda of disbelief, doubt and dirt
    Clean Up TV!
            Ocular labia framed
            in the wide-angled narrative.
            Prophet come prude,
            shrill against the normative effect
            of full penetration.

projected into millions of homes through the television screen.
    Clean Up TV!
            The director general of our morality,
            permissive's equal and opposite reaction.
            Pulling at the roots of filth,
            she keeps the dirt censored under her nails.
            Terrier in a twinset, her pearls
            cast before swine.

Rem Acu Tetigisti   Phill Jupitus/Porky the Poet

Bertie Wooster what a toff!
David Cameron what a toff!
Bertie Wooster old Etonian
David Cameron old Etonian
Bertie Wooster gets into scrapes
David Cameron gets into scrapes
Bertie Wooster doesn't work
But David Cameron
Doesn't work

Bertie Wooster went to Oxford
David Cameron went to Oxford
Bertie Wooster upset the police
David Cameron upset the police
Bertie Wooster he's got millions
David Cameron he's got millions
Bertie Wooster doesn't work
But David Cameron
Doesn't work

Bertie had a run in with Roderick Spode
David had a run in with Nigel Farrage
Bertie got shot of Honoria Glossop
David got shot of Rebekah Brooks
Bertie's catchphrase is 'What ho!'
David's catchphrase is 'Let me be clear about this.'
When Bertie's stumped he turns to 'Jeeves'
When David's stumped he turns to 'Osborne'
Bertie Wooster doesn't work
But David Cameron
Doesn't work

Irony Doesn't Exist   Robin Cairns

So sarcasm is the lowest form of wit?
Well, I scraped again at the barrel of comedy's awful bottom
And lower still found…irony

Or did I?

Warren Mitchell bought a nice bungalow, thank you very much
From playing Alf Garnett
'Send them back!' he girned, 'Taking our jobs.'
Out here in tellyland we felt for Dandy Nicholls,
loved the Scouse Git, fancied Una Stubbs
'It's the blacks!' said Alf
Warren got angry when people bawled in the
street, 'You tell 'em, Alf! Good on you!'
'The joke's on you…' Warren would fizz.
'The joke's on idiots like you!'

Dark nights in that sumptuous bungalow did Warren ever groan
That the sussed and clever audience on whom irony depends
To 'get it'
Were horribly outnumbered
By those who didn't

It's the hazard of high-minded comedy
That your crafted knowing parody gets taken at face value
And you wind up retired in a bungalow paid for
By the approval of those pleased to see
opinions you despise given air

But ironic? No, I'm afraid not
Not for piquant incongruity.
Warren's wealth through bolstering bigotry may be incongruous
but the bungalow he bought was not piquant. It was nice.
Nor ironic by aping ignorance for comic effect

The high-minded types who like to smirk at ignorance
all switched off appalled by the clueless script
Leaving only those who agreed with Alf
Mirthlessly

What happened to Warren though, through Alf, was sad
And it's not irony when someone sets out to do
something worthwhile…then miserably fails

There is the final ironic, the sense of highlighting
human folly. Warren certainly achieved that.
His own
But that means irony is just poignancy…for cruel people
No, I found in humour's abysmal butt nothing beneath sarcasm
When the sussed and the clever are watching *Panorama*
Irony doesn't exist

Intermission 1

FERRERO ROCHER

Ferrero Rocher   Lesley Ingram

We bob under cobwebs laddering the space
between desiccated tomato plants, dead air,

down the aisle to your workbench
where your life is offered up to us

transparent, labelled, shelved and boxed
in perfect plastic caskets. Lolly sticks,

dibbers, ties, bobtails, seeds, coiled string—
the silence is shattered by dropping pennies

and your voice Don't spend much on me.
The smallest box will do. Those Ferraris. Please.

DOMESTOS

Domestos   Cathy Bryant

So is there, deep in Germland, a memorial
to The Unknown Germ? To the escapees,
unlike those poor known germs who are killed
not just a bit, but dead, in a dull thud of tautology.
Just one squirt—Flash, boys, Flash! No, worse—
Domestos, mowing them down like soldiers
and all they can do is hope that there's an afterlife
with divinely filthy, Harpic-less harps.

Hamlet Cigars Jacqueline Thompson

Behold the baldy man's conceit, the way he flourishes his wee
   comb,
daintily coaxing the last, lank tendrils across his boiled-egg pate.
Watch how he flaunts his Scottish teeth, eyebrows arching coyly
as the seconds stretch. We know what *surely* happens next.
Just when he stoops that streaky heid FLASH goes the humbling
   camera.

Just when that simper slips FLASH goes the shaming lens.
Look how it chastens him even as the stool descends! But then:
the rasp of a match, a nimbus of smoke, an emanation of Bach
as if from paradise. See, it's posers who parade the frailest hide,
and it's the little things that help restore our pride.

PG Tips Michael Scott

Give the monkeys an infinite number of
pianos and they won't get them down
the stairs. Those chimps chew gum instead of drinking tea.

Chewing gum—not talking—not moving pianos
but they love to ripple their human rubber faces and say
'It's the taste' even when it isn't
even when Mr. Shifter has a bad back
and just wants a banana
or a letter from his family
back in the Congo.

Part II

From Africa, Out   Ric Hool

Tropos,
      a turn, twists away, its force
a tornado: the brickwork comes apart.

        From ruin we go
          forward

into space in fashion of Northern Lights
or stars burning bright across eye-caught skies.

Always the Men Morris of Misrule
untie the dance, unstring its tune
to filch from the hat to thirst
                  at drinkless bars.

In poem, in picture
by a stream, his body hacked,
fallen from the charts,
from boogie-woogie popped dreams
Pindar hears Orpheus scream the blues,
'Hell grants what love seeks'
reverberated in empty rock n roll wardrobes.

That spiral to now and on...

              'C'mon baby, let's do the twist.'

The Tango   Ian Parks

When Valentino danced it on the silent silver screen
the women swooned and fainted in the aisles.
The thin-lipped mouth, the black and darting eyes,
the stamping boots and waistcoat of a Latin matador

proved too much for the unsuspecting wives
accustomed to the foxtrot, the cha-cha and the waltz
who drank poison by the hundred, slashed their wrists
or jumped from Brooklyn Bridge, the Empire State

finding life was not worth living when he died.
So clench the reddest rose between your teeth
and curl a sheer black calf around my thigh.
I'll march you up and down the parquet floor,

the band blindfolded in a room of potted palms.
Surrender to a passion you know can't be denied
and dance the tango—it takes two—
the dance of love, the dance of suicide.

Catching Catwoman   Angela Readman

The night lays saucers of milk in rain potted yards.
Kitchen doors twitch, tails of light in the dark.

I think whips; strung across the moon, a clothes line
is a scalpel opening an eye. We're all trying

to catch Catwoman, dump her suit on a doorstep
again, wash her life story in streetlight like bleach.

I don't know how to make the bad into a suit that fits.
I do not know the amount of lives a woman can live,

if they equate with the numbers of lovers who left.
She has feathered a bed of their sleeping heads,

the mouths of the loved are robin breasts, ripen a yawn.
It can't be so hard to learn to leave love in a litter-box,

steal another dream, mould our spiky backs into another
warm open palm. Quiet as the bones mice, slippers pad,

we all wait for something, someone to claw her way out
of the sack of another night that drowns our young- the girls

we once were, whoever it was we thought we'd become.

The Dynamics of the Dandelion Duo   Gerry Potter

So there's me and my nephew
who's one year younger,
and will be at my side all my life.
Robin, cape is smaller,
yellow, but he's no coward.

Our Gotham is tenement, Autumn.
We've got the post war red-brick
ghosts of ancestors, hugging.
Standing on the grave of too many people
and an air-raid story.
Hands on hips, cloaks a billowing.

With fingers shading our eyes
we search for super villains.
We protect the red brick.
Protect the ghosts.

At six, all the air bristling
with story-telling and adventure.
Spirit of the old man,
the witch on the ground floor
and Nicknackynoona disturbed on his bike.

There's gunpowder and the dandelion n' burdock plot afoot.
We'll solve it.
The Joker won't drink it and packets of crisps, will be reward.

It's in the grit
the charcoal where the bon-fires blazed,
broken glass and bits of earring, Double Diamond beer mats.
In the yell of our mothers shouting.
'Never mind Batman and Robin, John and Gerard, It's time
    for tea.'

Me And Dave And Thelonius Monk Waiting For The 14 Bus   Ian McMillan

Another Friday evening in Dave Sunderland's front room.
Another new LP bought in the jazz section of Casa Disco.
Another night when Dave's mam was out at the Chapel.

Turn it up, Dave, turn it
Right up. Turn the lights out, Dave
And let's wait.

Another track on the Underground album: Ugly Beauty.
Another rearrangement of time and space and coincidence.
Another listen, Dave. Put it on again, mate. Soon be time.

In the front room dark
We try to snap our fingers
And it sounds like rain on a soft roof.

Another few moments to wait, if the 14 bus is on time.
Another double-decker light/modern jazz moment.
Another adolescent evening spent wishing we could leave here.

Round the corner by The Station Inn,
The 14 bus; Monk's music redefines
So much, so much. The 14's lights light
Up the room, sweep over it, away.

Another hour to wait before the next 14 bus, Dave.
Another biscuit from the tin. Let's pretend it's a whisky biscuit.
Another magical moment, Dave: Thelonious, the 14, the light.

Play it again, until your mam
Comes in. She said she was bringing chips
And mushy peas. We'll pretend they're
Jazz peas, Dave; jazz peas.

John Coltrane   Rodney Wood

I watched dancers bouncing to the beat
and planting their feet to the classics
I Will Survive, Stayin' Alive, I Feel Love,
Heaven Must Have Sent You, Good Times,
Born To Be Alive, and *Don't Leave Me This Way.*
Next morning I cleaned up their debris
of pants, flat trainers, butt ends, sweet packets,
breast pads, pink towels, stag and hen costumes
and once, an urn holding chaotic ashes.
For my efforts I was paid in classic albums
including a copy of *A Love Supreme.*
But being white, middle class and from Aldershot
I could never understand the yawps and squawks
of racism and how the church and gospel
were wrapped tightly round everything
like a DNA molecule. Even so I listened
to the Trane album with the volume way up
so I could feel the colours and sounds
run through my body with the burning
urgency that took me to another world
where I needed more oxygen, more supplies
and someone to lead me by the hand.
Liver cancer took him, John was made a Saint
but came back from the dead to receive a lifetime
achievement award and ascended into heaven
holding a precious horn that could explode
with all the notes in the known universe.

Portrait of Tony   Alison Grant

Try charcoal, something half-burnt, soft,
that quickly casts a shadow on the canvas.
His shoulders, smooth and round, occupy
most of the space, lean forward
to push aside
heavy air.

His chin is tucked against his neck
sunk within the collar of a short sleeved shirt,
his hands play the cards, flick
and grip, the knuckles always white
as if letting go's
too easy.

There is no trace of his mother,
except that his mouth is ready not to smile,
while his eyes check out the pool, reflect
the ducks, their direct line of flight,
the way they find their feet
on water.

Nobody's perfect, especially not you   Claire Trévien

You're no speakeasy saxophonist, Joe.
you're a borrowed costume,
a collage made for two.

Shrug on the suit of a bachelor, Joe.
Take your monochrome morals
and clip on the ears of an innocent listener.

You're no sweet end of the lollipop, Joe.
when you pack up a dress
or your fugitive locks.

Your shadow shirks bullets like a promise to call, Joe.
Your eyes are the only escape
route I can't trust.

You kissed Sugar Kane like you invented ice cubes, Joe,
but it was your Josephine that I liked
before you peeled off her lipstick and threw it in the deep.

Why did you erase her, Joe?
You're melting at the bottom of the glass
like backwash in the ocean.

Pac Man's Last Stand   Andrew Philip

We funt him dossin in a piss-scented close
oot the back o a defunct arcade,
his canary coupon dulled fae dool and stour
tae say naething o the bargain booze he swallied
fae a bottle happed in a broun paper poke.

He telt us his wife had run aff wi Super Mario.
Nou, he wis dinin on the dustbins, dwinin awa
for want o a pouer pill and a braw sheenie cherry;
in a constant, feartie, blootered dwam
o Inky, Binky, Pinky and even Clyde closin in

for the kill. Haurdly a shaddae o his auld sel.
The worst o it wis, every time he yawned
his gub wid gant that wee tait wider till it seemed
he'd fauld in on hissel and the air aroun him growe
shairp wi thae twa wirds ilka gamer dreids.

Naiturally, we taen him hame wi's and fed him up
on spare fou stops, Morellos and tartrazine.
Man, ye shuid hae seen thon appetite!
The trouble stairted wi a toattie bite taen oot
the sofa. Afore lang, the living room was a guddle

o sawdust, torn swatches and chowed wires. I'm gey feart
he'll suin hae eaten us oot o hous and hauld.
And that's whaur youse come in. A puckle wee ghosties
dinnae fleg me, but yon yellae golach's anither story.
The doors and windaes is aw locked. He'll no suspect a thing.

The Names   Andrew Fox

At midnight,
a balloon drifts past my window;
it gives off
a frosty luminescence
and beneath
the gorgeous envelope of starlight
hangs a black gondola
in which
my foe sits and watches me,
through his telescope.

His name, like my own,
is Jeremy Paxman.
He is the one
who usurped the name
granted me by the devil
to realise
the long plunge downward
of his glimmering career.

What more does he want?

The silk parachute
that belongs to him, or the one name
I must protect above all others:
the name of the child
who is active in eternity,
who speaks to god
and is not ashamed?

Jackie Wilson's Love...   Brian Whittingham

lifted me higher,
in a stowed *Sgt. Peppers* nightclub
where the mirrored walls pulsed
where condensation rivulets
formed raindrop patterns.

Jackie Wilson's love...

lifted me higher,
in the packed *Electric Gardens*
where us 60s hippies
with our patched denims, granddad vests, desert boots
and our courage fuelled
by four shilling pints from the Griffin bar
danced the steps of our teenage aspirations

that we still sometimes dance
in our minds when we listen to Jackie
on our iPods instead

of our listening booths of the past
in the 23rd. Precinct record store
where the black shiny vinyl spun our dreams
indelibly into the youth of our minds.

Jackie Wilson's love lifted,
and still keeps lifting me...

Higher, higher and higher!

Letter to Jocky Wilson from Svalbard
(after Sid Waddell)   Stevie Ronnie

The English poison the water.
> —Jocky Wilson's Nana

Here too, the tradition is abandoned mines
and in this tar orange photograph of you
your twenty-one gram arrow competes

the later stages of the Butlins tournament.
Pints swill glorious cheers yark.
I understand the loosing of your teeth

on the back of Gran's stubbornness
at the Grand Master's semi-final
and how gestures are the fuel of Wallsend.

But the doubles and trebles had the better of you.
I am locked in your dressing room with two cans
and cheese sandwich crumbs in my hair.

In there I see the orphanage in your eyes
(the address of which you gave the sergeants)
and your Nana's words, dear John Thomas Wilson.

Blow Rico Blow   Jim Carruth

Because the message can be black and white
ebb and flow of bodies heaving in the night

booted, suited driftwood of youthful rage
join with the band, overflow the stage

ska's beat translation sparks release
from thatcher, dole queues and police

dance floor's muscular bone on bone
sweats rude boy transfusions in 2-tone

dead pan terry spitting words of hurt
to pork pie hat, fred perry shirt

for all the skinheads, mods and punks
those lost forgotten teenage drunks

the debris of the sick and broken
music is an anger spoken

the tale untold beneath the facts
for those who fall between the cracks

night clubs and streets the only choice
for lovers left without a voice

despair keeps dancing skin on skin
that dark in dammer's toothless grin

rico rodriguez pick up your horn and blow
Blow Rico Blow.

Factory Records   Rob A. Mackenzie

Ultimately, Factory could only have survived on
sound economic principles, and it didn't have any.
That was the whole charm of it.—Peter Saville

The leeches were living, dead and in charge,
grasping music as income and expenditure.
Thatcher's bouffant helmet was a sprayed shell
the New Romantics sidled into like crabs,
clawing and acquisitive—the novelty virtues.

Factory peddled contracts signed by drunks
on disposable napkins, fused music and art
for bedrooms. Who could forget Section 25
or Crispy Ambulance? Men in yellow trunks,
women outdoors in Spring, that's who...

The fans stayed indoors until Chicago House
hit the north. Property boomed beyond control:
Madchester's hottest club, gangster bouncers,
death by ecstasy, suicide, cancer and smack,
law suits, two massive bands (massive bills).

Who could forget Northside or Crawling Chaos?
Don't answer. Lapses are painful. Fourteen years
with no business plan was almost miraculous:
flowers for staff daily, the florists left unpaid.
Entertainment in spades until the charm ran out.

Vastly Improved By Sudden Death   Andrew J. Wilson
—after E. E. Cummings

those Sex Pistols
(deceased)
       fortyfive
       calibre boys from Kingdom
                    Come
who(')re into onetwothreefourfivesix D!sT0rT!0N
                          fuck me

that's the way to do it
            and what i want to know is
how do you like your bastard kids
Mister Punch

          (and)

sixteenandtwothirds
      thirtythreeandathird
            fortyfive
                 seventyeight
                         revolutionsperminute

the nights were long
            but the years were too damned short
ever get the feeling
          you've been cheated

          (or)

if there'll always be an England
will the contents
      settle   mark

          during   question
              transit

The Last Gang In Town?   Tony Walsh

Who, these days, are the rebels worth the name?
Who hates the army, hates the RAF?
Who, these days, takes a gutter sniper's aim?
Who fights the law with every beat and breath?

Who, these days, has the baselines or the balls?
Who's sussed and struts where white man fears to tread?
Who, these days, answers back when London calls?
Who catches fire and burns like Natty Dread?

Who'll wave a flag above the shit parade?
Who'll educate and agitate the youth?
Who'll use guitars as weapons, unafraid?
Who'll rock the very casbah with the truth?

Come, stand and fight; together, not alone.
Go, start a fucking riot of your own.

Camp Freddy's Lament   Andy Jackson

We haven't talked like this for years—was it '68?
Those frantic minutes on the mountainside,
the world see-sawing, undecided. The weight
was always shifting, but a cataclysmic slide
was coming, in Paris or some other failed state.

The optimist in all of us was so preoccupied
with endings that we never thought to look
at how the Fifties changed the rules. Besides,
the public never had the time to read the book
and therefore only had the movies as a guide,

where their idea of a heist was Holloway
and Guinness with their phoney Eiffel Towers.
Ambitious, yes, but trust the script to underplay
the menace, not a gun in sight for two hours,
possibly the reason why they almost got away

with it. We took that London charm to heart,
where villains did the right thing by their mums,
but soon we learned you had to look the part,
Anderson & Sheppard suits, king of the slums
but still not knowing *a la mode* from *a la carte*.

So, if you want to know what happened next,
if the promise of a great idea came and went,
all I can reveal is what you probably expect—
we never really worked it out, and this lament
was bagged along with all my personal effects.

In the absence of a sequel, or a post-credit reveal
I can tell you; there never was a driver at the wheel.

Mansfield-Reservoir Dogs   Deborah Tyler-Bennett

Take dark-finned hire cars, trains and buses
to one-horse towns, without said hosses.

Re-directed by Shane Meadows,
see them striding, slowest motion,
suits thin as plotted good-intentions,
revenge Jim Thompson-plan away.

Mr Off-White, Pinkish, Trackie-Blue,
showing at a *Yates's Lodge* near you.

Shades read *Parmarni, Guci, Ray's Bans,*
eyes behind glower: 'what yo' lookin' at?'
Grim times breed desperado-clichés,
shadows big as pay-day promises.

Schemes noted on old bookies' slips,
hair, tight-fat in pan of chips.

Reflected in *Poundland* windows,
white-shirted intent scanning *99p Paradise,*
Carousel, Sell-By-Special,
Bet with the Betting King.

Mayhem razor-bites away from
Skeg, terraces, basement;
steps round chairs perfected
at *Northern Soul* nights.

Inglorious bastards, band apart,
train, bus, dark-finned car then out

or would be, if time hadn't stitched-them-up
lips tightening like filmic paper-cuts.

Split   Agnes Marton

'Indestructible, ha!,' moaned the shrink in a real-time yawn.
'Jack Ba-u-er. Like the guy yesterday called Dionysos.'

Demons closer and farther,
Luring me. Swishing tick-tock,
waves around. Hollow Dream Beach,
time-bubbles popping goose-flesh.

>   Let's get something straight, no games,
>   or I will rip your tongue, kid,
>   you gonna tell me what-whatnot,
>   I'm not messing with you, full stop.

Spectral, spongy sheets: choice shore,
random corridors, I'm lost;
or am I building up step-lead,
mundane, sacrifice-verge slot?

>   Mistakes, so many... I thought
>   I'd have time to correct all.
>   Shoot, I shoot you back. One, two...
>   or (gut instinct) I'll break your wrist.

Am I in transition towards
your splitscreenous distance?
Answers deeper and softer,
almost, hard-to-reach, not yet.

'The longest day of my life,' thought the shrink. For a nice
      change,
he watched a whole season of 24 in one sitting, biting his nails.

Bourne   Jan Dean

crowds are savannah
each walker a tall stem
moving in the rhythm of the wind
in step with them he is invisible
gold skin in gold grass

when he watches he waits
break rank and
click
he locks on
he is us broken and betrayed
the beautiful monster
trying to get back to Eden

every window a rabbit hole
each hatch and heating duct
a loop in the labyrinth
light running
in fibre optic cables
wound him
and he'll bring you hurt

the iron sea suckled
at his slow leak of blood
now he takes the world
for his weapon

Visit to Tracy Island   Lucy Jeynes

After we'd watched the wrestling
Had a nice cup of tea (two sugars)
We'd talk about where to go on holiday.
The conversation always went the same:
Every year I begged for Tracy Island
And ended up at Pontins, Camber Sands.

However hard I willed it
Dad's rosebushes did not fall aside
When the Triumph backed out the garage.
Even now I can draw you a plan
Correct in every detail from
Retractable pool to rocket pad.

We could not go abroad, as Grandad
Crossed the Channel in 1944
And that was quite enough.
Then—miracle—at Whitsun
We were off to the Isle of Wight.
Countdown days and Thunderbirds Are Go.

I made myself a badge and sash
Drew up designs for planes and submarines
In case we'd have to hurry to the rescue.
Turns out every island is different
And looking for Lady Penelope
You might find Queen Victoria instead.

The almost great escape Anne Connolly

Reverend Father Jack here
checking back to Craggy Hell
after three weeks in a Dublin cell
for, I have been well informed,
disgraceful drunkenness
and the concomitant
unseemly language
which, it is maintained,
I pepper-pot without restraint.

How quaint, when all I use
is the accepted variation
on the act of copulation.
A fly vowel-slip that here in Éire
we have honed to a merry quip
in the most common of parlance.
It rhymes so perfectly with heck
which is, after all, the eschatalogical
expletive favoured by my more
fastidious brethren and the nuances
of which theology I have not yet
depleted in this particular hell—
Dougal the deranged and prizzy Ted
but most of all that dizzy Doyle
wed to a perpetual vow of tea.
'Won't you have another Father…
aaaaahhhhh sure go on, go on!'

Well indeed I will! For is it any wonder
that when my wits are sundered
I have occasionally fled into a superior
distillation? My own golden stream
that hides a Munchian scream…

'Aaaaaaaaaaaahhhhhhhhhhhhhhhh!!!!!!!'

Colonel Kurtz   Jim Stewart

A third of the way in
to Conrad's thicket,

he knows you're coming.

Hack further. Disentangle Coppola's lines
—pitch black, Wagnerian.

He's expecting you.

His third of the sea is blood. From his pit,
stinging locusts, with human faces.

His river is wormwood. Steer upstream,
where its bitter head's

dark lantern, crescent
moon face in shadow,

spells damnation's alphabet
simply, so you can follow.

He's never not been ready.
As you must,

hack his heart's jungle. Swing that machete.
Murder your image.

Pugwash addresses a weevil   Jo Bell

Command is an unfriendly thing.
Count your blessings, little stowaway.
Your crewmates are united, labouring

to eat, to rest, to mate, to worm their way
into another simple dynasty, another barrelful
of biscuit; whilst I must raise my telescope to see

another graceless cretin tumble from the mainsail,
botch a reef knot, snag the anchor, take the piss.
The Black Pig's hold is full of pearls and ridicule.

They've no respect, these men. They're ignoramuses.
If mermaids fetched up—phosphorescent, slick
and muscled in our wake, silver-glossed as fish—

then Master Mates would rush to fuck
or to harpoon them. Every man unschooled,
unshod, each cutlass blunt and not a book

between them. Not one plays backgammon.
My floury friend, I've no companion to soothe
this poop-deck agony. The monumental ocean,

hornpipe sea; perpetually in motion, still unmoved.

The Dying Words of Patrick Moore   Paul McGrane

The Martians
live
in houses
just like yours

with chimney
roof
four windows
and a door

Instead
of humans
Martians
live inside

I may
have said
they don't exist
I lied

Less is Moore   Niall O'Sullivan

According to his autobiography,
Roger Moore got pissed for the first time
at the pub opposite the Brockwell Lido

and staggered back to Stockwell in time
to join his parents in the shelter,
passing out before the first bombs fell.

Imagine if trajectories had veered off course
and the payload's slide whistle
had ended it there and then—

a bobby's son still dropping his Ts
before RADA spooned them back into his gob?
Then perhaps a troop of better men

could have idled beneath Templar's halo,
commandeered a hover-gondola through Venice
or neutered a nuke while dressed as a clown;

but none would have worn their countenance
as a knowing manifesto on culture—
highbrow, lowbrow, sod all that crap in the middle.

Benny's Crossroads Blues   Martin Figura

*Benny went up a ladder in 1987 to put up Christmas
decorations and was never mentioned again.*

Benny woke up this morning, fell down to his knees,
begged the Lord for mercy, 'have mercy if you please
for Miss Diane she lay dyin', dyin' of a brain disease.'

Miss Diane didn't wake up this morning, her livin' wasn't clean.
'Open up the gates Lord, they've turned off her life-support
    machine.'
But the devil was on reception, he picked up that telephone:

'Crossroads Motel, can I help you, can I take your soul,
for that's the price I'm askin', down here in the hole.'
Miss Diane she lay dead and the day was getting cold.

She'd slept with men from Solihull and that can take its toll
and cause a girl to ramble down by the old canal,
gaze into dark and wonder—how far she could fall.

'Lucifer I love her and some take me for a fool
and though my soul is simple, my heart is very bold.'
The sky it cracked open and Benny sold his soul.

Now we rise and we are everywhere is written on a stone
she danced and called to the devil beneath a pale pink moon,
now Miss Diane she sleeps there and the path is overgrown

If you live in Birmingham, then you can sing The Blues.
Benny sang a lonesome song, Miss Diane was his muse
and every step he takes now is in the devil's shoes.

He's climbed Jacob's ladder, his arms aglow with tinsel
while his soul burns down below, where the howl
of Amy Turtle's Hoover shakes the walls of that motel

*'Now we rise and we are everywhere' is the epitaph on Nick Drake's
gravestone in the village where Crossroads was filmed.*

We're All in Our Private Trap   Josephine Scott

She hasn't noticed the silhouette moving behind her,
feels just a suspicion of air stirring, and the shower
curtain sticking to her legs like wet cabbage.

Shivers as she thinks of the birds
throwing swooping shadows on the walls,
their glass eyes interrogating her, instilling remorse.

Lets the pounding water wash the image
of approaching cars out of her mind, their beams
shining searchlights, and telegraph poles

standing like crucifixes across the horizon.
The shock comes suddenly, cold steel intensifying regret,
producing a frenzy of images; a life she'd hoped for.

She snatches at the shower curtain as if grasping
for the past, the hooks popping empty promises,
realises that you can't buy off unhappiness.

Everything turns black as icy needles scratch
against her skin, dragging her guilt anticlockwise
down the drain, dark as chocolate sauce.

1981: Kraftwerk? Ja, Danke Valerie Laws

Kraftwerk at Newcastle City Hall. They are the future,
Like robots singing love songs to machines. They
Are the anti-matter to more earthly stars—it's all
About them, not being about them. We get it. So cool
To be cold. Teutonic, perfect, disciplined, yet something
Joyful, yearning, troubled filters through the synthesised
Sound, as if computers have souls. I wear flying suits. I
Am the future too, borrow farmer friends' overalls at first
Until boutiques catch up with me. We dance like robots,
Our faces blank, our actions repetitive as our music. Decadent
Yet mechanical, our nightclubs are Roman orgies re-created
On Saturn. We long to see the band, part of me still expects
Heavy metal's love me, fuck me, stage-front writhing
But they are at the back lined up like showroom dummies,
Their neon name-boards taking centre stage. They play.
The music's perfect, nothing distorted but the band themselves.
Each stands beside his replica; eight androids. Strobe lights
    flicker,
Making real men fake and models seem to move. Just once,
With tiny instruments on palms they venture to the front, play
Pocket Calculator. Then into the pause before applause a yell,
Human, joyful, yearning from our ranks: 'I love you, Florian!'

All four freeze, almost shyly scuttle back behind their consoles
As the crowd laughs warmly, a wave of love like radioactivity
Pursuing them off stage. I picture them sitting still, recharging,
Waiting for daylight, can't bear to imagine fags, porn mags,
Cans of lager, fart jokes in that tour bus. In my near future
On an autobahn in Sunderland I'm left part-metal with a robot
    walk.
Now decades on the technology to fix me, make me pain-free,
    perfect
As a machine still waits off stage. The tweeting android in my
    palm

Tells me Kraftwerk, three of them replicants, will be playing at
Tate Modern, but not, I hope, to the gallery. They are still the
 future.

Abba   Luke Wright

My my! It's nearly two am
the DJ spins one final hymn
the dance floor writhes with grins and limbs
sometimes it's good to just join in
Come and sing some ABBA.

A clumsy nursery rhyme plus score
of muzak from department stores
but still the hoards come back for more.
Leave your kudos at the door!
Come and sing some ABBA.

Fifteen? Painful? NME?
Slogging through a Fall LP?
Why not take a chance on me?
Let Prozac pop songs set you free!
Come and sing some ABBA.

The lyrics, yes, they're gleaming turds
the blandest cliches ever heard
the syntax duff, the rhymes absurd
but LOOK, the whole place knows those words
Come and sing some ABBA.

ABBA-Yabba-dabba-do
a level up from Agadoo

I've just rhymed 'do' with 'do' with 'do'
this stanza is my Waterloo
Come and sing some ABBA.

Divorce, of course, the pop machine
but still, their songs were cake and cream
from car to club to stark canteen
unleash your inner Dancing Queen
and come and sing some ABBA.

Fanny Cradock   Anne Berkeley

Phyllis Primrose-Pechey
knew what it was to be poor,
cooked on a single gas ring,
sold hoovers door to door.

Her god was Auguste Escoffier,
her father wrote for the stage.
Nobody's nose was toffier
and nobody knew her age.

She cooked in tiara and ballgown
(an apron was just for the maid).
From her kitchen she scolded a nation
and kept them thrilled and afraid

as Johnnie, dapper, submissive,
chunked ice in another pink gin,
held the goose aloft on a carving fork
as if carving a violin:

a lament for the goose in fen honey
a lament for the oceans of fish
a lament for prawn cocktails and melon
a lament for the garnish and kitsch.

Smile for the camera, Fanny,
flourish your *savoir-faire*,
arch your *farceur*'s eyebrows,
doyenne of the scalloped hair.

Fame can sink fast as a *soufflé*
with a *moue* and a wave of the hand.
You're consigned forever to YouTube
where your final appearance is panned.

At the Fat Duck Judi Sutherland

Tonight we are serving loin of social climber
poached, *sous-vide,* with hubris vinaigrette
and a garnish of toasted clever-clever;
a slice of banker's bonus wafted past your table
on a cocaine-aromatic fifty pound note.

Let me present our signature dish, a fish
out of water, molecularly, a Maillard reaction—
we challenge traditional techniques
for gastronomical umami satisfaction.
Why not entertain our five-critic roast

of spatchcocked A A Gill
stuffed with Rayner, plucked and drawn
containing boned Fort *farci*
filled with prime Giles Coren and a final
tiny, quailing Parker-Bowles?

Here's a frothy little mousseline
of sweet self-consciousness on a silver spoon
popped into your optimal tasting orifice
by our expert front-of-house *degustationnaires*;
(I'm sorry if that took you unawares).

After dinner, we recommend you relax
in our refurbished vomitorium, its *chaises-longues*
of washable suedette; the décor has a witty
diced carrot theme. You may enjoy the songs
of food-bank Visigoths, marching to sack the City.

La Genèse de M. Hulot (pour Jacques)   Simon Barraclough
—Tati dit: Que la lumière soit! Et la lumière fut

The Big Bang, as we know,
didn't bang and wasn't big,
but flowered from infinitesimal
to a good thumb-sized pipeful
in the blink of an unevolved eye;
and we know that on the fifth day
Jacques made the fowl that fly
above the earth, and played them
like a Theremin with the Sun
(which he'd made earlier)
to sweeten the air with song;
and for the sake of divine comedy
he dubbed the sound on afterwards,
and fashioned then the human ear
for the click of rapid heel on floor,
the silent slamming-door, the gadgetry
of tragicomedy, the *rhubarb*
of a babbling Babel; and so began
his gallant dance, the fingertip on satin strap
so as not to stroke the tender back,
so as not to intervene.

Keaton in Space   W. N. Herbert

Since it is black and white and absolutely silent
since his death Keaton has been travelling between
the stars. At first he could pull railroad track out
of a carpet bag as far as Jupiter, where he fell
from the footplate of *The Great Leveler* into
exactly the blind spot of the eye of the Red Spot.

As he fell he replaced each pork pie hat torn from
his head with a pork pie hat he rapidly fashioned
from a normal hat using a thick paste of sugar water,
clapping it onto his head as soon as it dried only
for it to be removed at once by his terminal velocity
all the long while of miles of staring straight down.

Around him on all sides were stacks of jalopies
and paddle steamers whirling and crashing together,
hand-cranked cameras still turning, thickets of mikes,
lighting rigs like blazing sails on gyring schooners,
the fife-rail of one of which he hooked himself to
by a shoe-tip, and steered for Saturn's celluloid rings.

After a lonesome century pursuing himself by handcar
around their gritty circuit, getting so close sometimes
as to grab his own shoulder, only to shrug off
the distraction, he tired of the back of his own head
and boarded a giant eyeball, immersing himself
in salt jelly and embarking on night's longest stare.

After thousands of years of being dead, the *Beckett*
brought him forth from the Belt of Teleology,
and he forgot there ought to be a reason for
his voyaging, forgot he was anything but a beetle
rolling an eyeball from darkness to darkness,
and dreamed that he was filming this again.

Belfast Cowboy   Brian Johnstone

...down in the hollow, playing a new game.
—Van Morrison, *Brown Eyed Girl*

It wasn't Madam George who drew you
from the back to backs, it was the discs
your Da collected Stateside in Detroit,
fetched back along with that guitar
so, twelve years old, you had a band,
went into orbit with The Sputniks
round flea pits and the local hops.

Showbands in sleazy clubs bought off
the sponge and pail, the windowsill
no place for Ulster accent R'n'B, or so
the province said, recognising where
the beat would lead. *It's Them, not us!*
the cry back then. And here it comes:
the night, its caustic glory, you escaped.

No hold on Maritime Hotel or City Hall,
troubles lain in wait. To quit the streets'
dividing lines you split from Sandy Row
for Caledonia, a land not of this world
but of The Man. Out there: another street,
another choir, an orchestra to outplay
flutes or Lambeg drums with Celtic soul.

Sure, it was almost Independence Day
for you, a state of mind, but even more
a state of play. The tenor of your voice
took on a hunger you would not outdo.
In weeks you made your masterpiece.
Your radio was on, the wavelength set.
It's too late to stop now, you heard it say.

Val The Man   Tony Curtis

—*Walk tall, walk straight and look the world right in the eye.*
   Val Doonican, *Walk Tall*

I saw him once in the wing mirror of my father's car.
He was coming down O'Connell Street like a film star
Being waltzed along by twelve excited women.
'Who's that?' I asked my father.
'That's your man who sings *Walk Tall*.'

'Johnny Cash!' I said.
 'Not at all,' my father said,
'He's the lad who wears the pullovers.'

'Liam Clancy!'
'No, no, no. He's the chap with the rocking chair.'

'Luke Kelly!'
 'No, Luke has a bar stool. This lad's from Waterford.
He sings the old Irish songs like *Paddy McGinty's Goat*.'

'John McCormack!'
'Do they not teach you anything in school; sure he's dead years.
Your man's a big success in England. He has his own TV show.
He's the Irish Engelbert Humperdinck. He croons like
Bing Crosby or Perry Como. His name begins with V.'

'Van Morrison!'
'Not at all, Van's grey and grumpy.
He's bright and cheerful. Your mother likes him.
You hear her singing *Scarlet Ribbons* when she's polishing.'

With that, my mother sat into the car.
'Did you see him? Did you see Val Doonican?'
'*Val The Man*,' I said, brightening.
'That's right son,' she said, smiling 'Val's the man.'

'And there he is, off his rocker,' my father said.
Then my mother gave him the eye,
As if he had just cursed on a Sunday.

Caractacus Potts Will Kemp

Imagine him as your dad: grey hair, wide grin,
the crackpot inventions of an Edwardian Q;
down on his luck yet still greeting
you with *Gawd bless yer, me ol' Bamboo!*

One minute he's fleeing a thug with no hair,
the next hopping down the farm track
as if stung by a bee, smoke everywhere,
a fizzing rocket strapped to his back.

Life's a breeze for you in that windmill:
no chores on Sunday, allowed to skip school;
never once told to sit up straight or keep still.
He even gives you sweets instead of fruit.

But it's not all bliss: you and your sister scrap.
His solution? A trip to the beach—
songs like a team bus en route to the match—
then home where he sings you gently to sleep.

A black hat   Judith Taylor

That harsh face would never have been the hero.
Even when you smile you make saloon proprietors nervous,
and railway officials. What you want, you get:
the train that doesn't stop at Tucumcari stops for you.

You make the best of a bad job.
You say what everyone says in your position
—how boring it would be to be the good guy—and we believe
there's genuine enjoyment in that wolf smile
as you choose among your weapons.

Though you get to be a big wheel
it's still the same machinery, and you know it:
you know its tune. In the prison camp a choir sings
to mask the noise of your interrogations

and the broken heart you carry with you plays
a little tinny song that winds down
when it's time for another killing.
Still, you smile. A different take perhaps
but you've a part in a long tradition

lending gravity to a formula
we're not sure deserves it now, if it ever has.
What the hell. It's a living.
The reckoning just before the end
you don't fear

and even when you're justice
on the murderer, the madman, it's a black hat you wear
when you face him down.

a matter of top gun Morgan Downie

fine figures of men, all,
the rolls royce swagger of aviators,
silver screened and luminous,
a klaxon dash of dawn patrol flyboys.
marvell and raleigh tumble soft as rain
as david niven escapes unsilked,
his aircraft disintegrating in fire.
and you, stuck in the minor theatre
of national service, spud-peeler,
clay-footed, a drudge.

a fine figure of a man,
like you, no eyes for mcgillis,
only the stick, the safe confine
of cockpit. he shimmers in desert
whites, the modern apotheosis
of airman. you hold your breath
as he is oiled for games, struts
towel clad in the closeted don't ask,
don't tell echo of the locker room.
top gun, i am dangerous
how easy such phrases
slip into *not my son.*
you kohl his eyes with your fists.

a fine figure, that mantra
in every breath taken while you
fall uncaught through clouds
of a life not lived, to wash up
at the water's edge, strip away
the dead weight of uniform.
there in the dunes, a naked boy,
waiting, and you, fine figures…

The Most Effectual   Jane McKie

Where can a guy get a decent Tuna on rye round here?
Always grey wrappers and greasy onion rings.

Sometimes I'm so tired I could put my feet up
in one of these trashcans, no kidding, pull on PJs,
bang down the lid. Can you hear that din!
Could be Fancy-Fancy, he's the type to croon—
cat around town, cat on the tiles. Or Spook
who's so, like, a beatnik. *Like, cool, TC.*
Or Brain—no, not Brain, who'd struggle
with the words. Hmm...not Benny. Nice little guy,
but can he murder a tune! Is it you, Choo Choo?
Stop with the opera; it's time now for action—

Only sometimes I get so tired of the routines,
the usual patter—the *Dribble, Dabble, Drubble*;
tired of the charm, the tricks, the chase,
all the holes in the yarns we gang of grifters spin
as we pace the precinct, its fragrant yards
our jailhouse. But every penitentiary has its perks:
out the corner of my eye—a cop's peaked cap
at the phone again. Probably reading Time its rights:
unauthorised use of a police phone (that's a 1206);
insulting an officer (that's a 402, most often cited).

Love it or hate it, we're family. He's not a quitter,
I'll say that for Dibble. Take him out of New York,
he'd survive. Put me down anywhere but this city,
this big riverboat with its laws and its sweet
unspooling line of swindlers and marks,
and sometimes...sometimes, I wonder if I'd float.

Professional   Susan Wicks

You've practised this for weeks. In dreams
you've tied the sacerdotal apron-strings.
The M's electric ring of flame's
white-hot beside your waiting rack of knives.

You've hardly slept. The hunger in your brain
is filled with coulis, jus, medallions of lamb
that weep pink tears, a mango
offered up three ways, your three-in-one.

Carpaccio of salmon. Scallops. Ecrevisse
on a bed of samphire. Sea-bass vacuum-sealed
to swim itself immortal in a bath
of seething water, suddenly released

and plated up—and somehow more or less
than what you had in mind. Your heart's
awash with longing, fingers shake to place
a wisp of leaves the judges tease apart

and chew and swallow, each involuntary twitch
a secret language, every frown or nod
or eyebrow speaking silent tongues,
unmoved by hours of vigil, sweat or blood.

It's time. You dare to raise your eyes
to theirs, you almost risk a smile—
for this is you, this flesh that's cooked and dressed
for Monica to put before Michel.

I, Who Love Chairs   Annie Freud

hate this chair,
so professorial, so of its time,
so symbolic,

and the theme tune,
suggesting executions
with its edgy pageantry,
and suggesting modernity
with its touch of Ravel.

I walk the diagonal path
into the spotlight.

My chosen subject is Baudelaire,
Les Fleurs du Mal, Jeanne Duval,
Eugène Delacroix, Gaspard Nadar,
The Painter of Modern Life.
Mon semblable,—Mon frère!

Shaggy and Scooby Doo   Andrew C Ferguson

Oh Scooby, my Scooby, where are you?
The old gang is gone:
Fred and Daphne split up, after two kids,
the girl just like her, but the boy
looks just like you. Who
would have thought it,
Scooby, Scooby Doo?

Ou sont les Scoobies d'antan,
now the old gang is gone?
Velma spiked her hair, sports tiny specs,
lectures to the eager boys at MIT,
but still wears those bright orange polo neck jumpers
—without you, she hasn't a clue.
But where are you, Scooby, Scooby Doo?

Stop all the clocks,
and take off the masks
of the money men with monsters below.
Now the old gang is gone, and there's no hide nor hair
of you, Scooby Doo, who
went off to Hollywood, for fortune and fame,
but the movie, it just wasn't true to you, Scooby Doo.

With the Scoobysnax stacked at the back
of the old abandoned mineworkings
still I wait for you,
Scooby, Scooby Doo.

Andy Pandy: Judgement Day   Matt Harvey

—Andy Pandy costumes are available on the internet to buy or rent

People forget.
The original Andy Pandy was a marionette
worked by string.
He looked a little like a young John Lydon.

Who did you look like, Andy?
A young John Lydon.

He lived in a picnic basket with his friend, Teddy
and Looby Lou—whom he never met.
People forget.

Did you ever meet Looby, Andy?
No.

If you see a grown man dressed as
Andy Pandy, please remember:
it's illegal and unethical
to punch him, even once.

But you can say, if you need to:
You there, in the stripey onesie,
yes you, dressed as Andy Pandy—
like an iced-up filo pastry,
like a seed-pod stuffed with smugness—
this is not enchanting whimsy,
all excuses are too flimsy.
Dump the jumpsuit, it's revealing
far more than it is concealing.

Alternatively you could form
an acapella group and sing:

Time to grow up, time to grow up
Dignity's waving goodbye
Goodbye

Mods   Wayne Holloway-Smith

On slender blue scooters they come, singing,
>   *There's love and disaster*
>   *Moving where our minds are at.*
Sometimes they add a little *bah-ba-ba-ba-ba-la-bah* in
   parenthesis.
Sometimes not. There has never been a more perfect set
of haircuts. Never before a less impressive set
of gangsters, careful-stepping *À bout de souffle.*
Flick knives and pill heads are so beautiful in this context.

The greatest mod I ever met was a man called Denzil. In his
   mind
he figured himself a poet. He washed dishes in a hotel backroom,
and his hair every Thursday. He wore his cuffs symmetrically
   rolled.
The best mods are alive in metaphors, walk in West End
   narratives,
and shebeens, and do violence with greasy bags of chips.
                          All day, actual poets,
like school kids, dream about sex, and sit about cafes
with dunked soldiers and egg yolk, sometimes they write things
   down.
Occasionally, they dream of a city overrun by singing mods,
get distracted and end up humming.

A girl with a café au lait in a film once said that poetry
is a way of inhabiting the world that you want.
She said it better than that.

Goths   Jack Little

An older kid called 'Uncle Syd' ran a profitable trade
in cigarettes behind Drama Block, wearing a wide brimmed hat

and mascara. My first day of high school: hearsay spread
talk of devil worshippers who danced around bins

and some said they made daytrips to
funerals. In musty woodwork class,
I saw etched on backpacks with black lipstick,   'I ♥ Marilyn'

Manson of course, but I thought of Monroe. Life rolled on:
hormonal and sweaty. A small-town boy, I trembled at myth,

at fragile monsters, had nightmares of forgetting my PE kit,
a golden era of confusion: fit in/stand out

each a disappointment, for no matter what the cult or clique;
goth, sporty, chav or chic

we were all lost in a vast sea of other frightened teens
just desperate to be part of something

Oral English   Sheenagh Pugh

Ichigoro Yuchida, keen to improve
his colloquial English, puzzles over

a text with his (equally baffled) teacher.
They can't seem to find *dolly old eek*

in the phrasebook. And why, during a shipwreck,
should Mr Horne laugh when our heroes

drag themselves up on deck? So many queries…
in the end, they think best to seek wisdom

from the writer, which is how they come,
courtesy of Mr Took, to knowledge

of some comic stereotypes, a secret language,
a national habit of wryness, a way of talking

as if one could make a joke of anything,
of code, of hiding from the law, of love.

Hancock's Half Hour   Pauline Plummer

The streets are cleared, a truce declared at home,
grown ups not shouting, in fits at all the jokes.
I don't get all the ranting of the glum
faced man tilting at windmills and mocked,
misunderstood for half-cock, naïve ideas,
his failures compost to a jibing wit.
He mirrors Dad's deluded hopes and fears,
aspiring to be middle-class and counterfeit.
Failure's a coin—on one side social shame.
He showed the sad man can't escape his class,
but he wanted more than simply entertain,
to be sublime, the flawless, comic genius.
He read and drank voraciously to find
answers for his troubled, desperate mind.

Sid's our Other, not post-colonial, but yet
different. We know the post war fifties type
translated into London, cranked to bet
a savvy tenner on the gee-gees. He waits,
stiletto ready, to skewer the humbug
of East Cheam. *Plenty ways to cocoa, schmooze,*
he tells our Tone in coat and Homburg.
I may be coarse but I get the tarts and booze.
Listen mate, he frowns his sun-dried, walnut phiz,
You haven't got a guinea or an ounce of sense.
You're a forelock tugging serf of Liz.
I'm the Empire's trickster, stripping the pretence.
We watched him fry pretensions to be toff,
our own cross-cultural bit of rough.

Judy McGuire

How many lost plaintiffs
grope begrudgingly
for impossible answers?
How tenuously
the small mind
clings to its claims.

Untrained breasts, flaccid excuses,
Judy cuts through 'baloney'
to the lean meat of the matter.
Sorts the cold facts that remain
subtracted from the spite that served it.

'Um is not an answer.'
'Beauty fades but dumb is forever.'
Deliver your judgements with that
Shiendlin shrewdness, pinched
with the salt of clarity
which serves the balance.

Old mensch, with your New York twang;
there's an audience for humiliation,
a world of strays who need
a Matriarchy for the misfits
who tolerates no chutzpah,
files them through row after row.

Millionairess arbitrator, oracle
whose judgements are golden.
You bank more per episode
than justice could ever claim.

Judge Dredd   Russell Jones

Forget everything that happened before.
It's the third Millennium. The world's changed.
I am not what you think I am: The law

giver, the hard lip, a bloody suit. War
grew the grunt in me, the dread, the rage.
Forget everything that happened? Before

the fallout I could have been so much more:
a boy, a dream, a lover, serene, sage.
I am not what you think I am. The law

was a way up, out, forward, another door.
Some careers advice that was! Assuage
for 'Take Everything.' That happened before—

every decade has its dog, its saviour
but a blinker's behind each cuff and cage.
I am not what you think I am. The law

is my cursed earth. It's true I've no rapport
but justice is my judge, my righteous gauge.
Forget everything that happened before,
I am not what you think. I am the law.

Black Lodge Recorder   Chris McCabe

A black box is a device which has input & output mechanisms. Its
internal workings are unknown. It is of the starling family & can
often be heard saying 'Leo, no!' Almost anything can be described
as black box, even the human mind. It is distinct for its wattled
feet. The opposite of a black box is a snow warbler chirruping in
porcelain. The death of a black box is often used in avant-garde
TV dramas to set the tone for the series: ludic but chilling. Most
black boxes now come pre-installed with Syrinx v.6. Although
these devices are omnivores—eating mainly insects & fruit—their
blood is redder than expected when it drips on an opened box of
doughnuts. Humans, to pacify their lust for displayed intelligence,
often attribute black boxes with names such as Waldo. Most species
nest in holes so lifetimes in cages exposes them to things they can't
forget. 'Leera, Leera; don't go there'. Sometimes they repeat these
things : 'hurting me'. Later models have developed extravagant
facemasks as if it to remain anonymous. They have two eyes that turn
clockwise to record & the voice licks itself strapped to black spools.
Even when the black box is shot with a bullet its voice remains
captured. 'Stop it, stop it. Leo, no!' Although called a black box
a black box is actually bright orange to make location easier after
a disaster. The orange is the same colour as a mynah bird's beak.

A Prisoner In My Own Home   John Hegley

We used to like Patrick McGoohan in Nineteen Sixties'
    Dangerman.
Him, the Special Agent stranger with the secret something and
    the quick fisticuffs.
Does Danger Mouse have anything to do with him?
When The Prisoner came onto our T.V. we tuned in on account
    of McGoohan.
The programme was odd, but we stayed with each week's new
    'Number Two' interrogator:
always a familiar face from elsewhere on our screen,
always a piece of theatre.
I wasn't so sure about the big white ball of vengeance that came
    in from the sea
but I went along with all the oddities, because it was McGoohan.

Thinking upon these matters, I suggested to my Mel,
that here was an example of an artist leading their public out of
    their comfortable confines
on the strength of achievements, more readily digested:
like The Beatles did with Magical Mystery Tour and the Yellow
    Submarine cartoon.
In response, Mel referred to another vintage cartoon creation,
    Mr Magoo
and adopting the tone of the short-sighted buffoon, quipped,
'Oh, Magoohan, you've done it again.'

SARAH LUND

Gudrun & Gudrun   John Challis

A shield to the Copenhagen winter is the wool
of hardy Faroe Sheep. Cold cases stain
the garment; a band of ashen snowflakes.
Sarah, should the piano key send you
in a dash for clues, as you cast your steely eyes
across the crime scene, and should one thread
snag itself on a branch or nail, and stitch
by stitch undo your jumper, then every turn

at which the knitter has misled us
will spill it, like a bad dénouement,
and we, armchair DCIs, Stieg Larsson books
akimbo, will know it's not the politician,
the superintendent or the father, will pin
it on the removal man, the partner,
or the businessman. It's all in the Gudrun
and Gudrun knitwear; a pile of wooly yarn.

Sailor Ripley Deputises for Ellen Ripley
Simon Barraclough

BISHOP
In nineteen minutes, this area's gonna be a
cloud of vapor the size of Nebraska.

RIPLEY
I wouldn't worry about that, Peanut. By then
people'll prob'ly be drivin' Buicks to the moon.

CUT TO:

RIPLEY
Did I ever tell you that this here space suit
represents a symbol of my individuality, and my
belief in personal freedom?

NEWT
About fifty thousand times!

CUT TO:

ASH
You still don't understand what you're dealing
with, do you? Perfect organism. Its structural
perfection is matched only by its hostility.

RIPLEY
Uh-oh!

ASH
I admire its purity. A survivor. Unclouded by
conscience, remorse, or delusions of morality.

                    RIPLEY
Peanut, you move me.

CUT TO:

                    BISHOP
It is impossible for me to harm or by omission of
action, allow to be harmed, a human being.

                    RIPLEY
Rockin' good news!

CUT TO:

                    RIPLEY
This is Sailor Ripley, last survivor of the
Nostromo, signing off. Stab it and steer!

Intermission II

Guinness   Roy Marshall

Not so much a pub as a palace of smoke and mirrors.
Not so much a request for a pint as the saying of a prayer.
Not poured as much as a sacrament unfolded in lace.
Not a wait for settlement but a suspended state of grace.
Not supped liquor but a dip through cloud to silk.
Not a drink so much as a delve beneath a creamed rim.
Not the backstreet bar but a seal slipping from rock to sea.
Not the low-lit booth but a blackbird swooping over a moonlit
    belfry.
Set it down, sure and steady as the foreleg of a jet black stallion
back in the paddock for a towel down after winning the Derby.

FAIRY LIQUID

Fairy Liquid   Irene Hossack

It was the lifestyle that I craved:
my six year old self imagined
my own mother discussing the virtues
of soft, smooth hands and gentle
long-lasting bubbles, with me
asking inane questions and mummy
replying with such graceful understanding.
Strong marketing and a soothing, hypnotic tune
had me longing for this kind of mother,
or at least one who bothered to wash up.

Hovis   Ruth Aylett

Do you remember your first
strawberry, warm from the garden?
Brown bread and honey that afternoon
of summer, and the smell of
cut grass in the evening?
No matter, this is what we are selling:
our bread of heaven,
a boy on a bike in shades of sepia
rattling down cobbles, with an
evocative tune. Better than memory.

Go Compare   Chris Riley

If we make a song and dance of it
then maybe it's too obvious,
comparisons are odious—

unless they're done with wit.
Plant a website in our memories
to compensate for injuries
we'd much rather forget.

We can make an operatic hit
go swirling round your memory
sung by a cartoon tenor in full, formal kit.

Part III

The Searchers   Tom Pow

My understanding so far—

that bitterness ruptures a man's
        narrative long after its cause has ended
that we'd follow some men, as we had once
        our fathers—when we knew our fathers
        by smell, like beasts
that once we knew our fathers as tamed,
        we needed other men we could follow
        into the dark brunt of life; such men
        as were careless of themselves, rare as leopards
that there are those who will not let go
        of whatever they fix on, be they hunters, artists
        or mystics; and among them, some won't see
        losing, even their lives, as defeat
that love and hate can be lit by the same flame
        and can bind in the same way; which is
        why we have to be guided by what lies
        between the two, by that which is nameless
that you stand on one side of the threshold
        or the other; on one side, the lamplit
        comfort of home and family; on the other,
        nothing—neither mountain, desert or rock—
        that cares; and that there is something
        noble in walking, knowingly,
        back into that brightness
and that there is also nothing—not a horse, a buffalo
        or a dog—lonelier than a man
        in the red dustscape of the world
that a philosophy lives or dies, not through
        erudition or skill in speech, but on the lips
        of who says it and by how they live it out
that life is its own agency and its purpose is
        to reveal the true nature of a man

or the true nature of a woman and this
can turn, in a moment, on an act of kindness,
compassion or love.

And is that then all there is to know?

That'll be the day.

UNFORGIVEN

Rider   Jan Dean

the trail ends begins
with graveyard mud and pigs
no high sierras   great plains
or rivers of bronze cattle running
down to Abilene

against longing and sense
he saddles up   rides
rises against a long horizon
becomes the sweep of the hill
and the shadow over it
moves beyond the price
that brought him here
beyond the lovely engineering
of the gun
into the dark morality
of vengeance

whoever owns the town
must understand
the land is still the land

Welcome to Royston Vasey   Angela Topping

Bab's taxi lurches down the high street, past
boarded-up Fleur de Lys with its gladioli ghosts,
round the Roundabout Zoo, watched by the angel
with his laurel crown, to collect a stranger
from the trembling train. Down at the job centre
Pauline clutches the pens, her only friends,
as jobseekers shuffle off to Dick Fisher's:
a flutter on the three o-clock passes dull afternoons.

In school they are doing Geography: lines and lines
and lines on a map, chanting places they will never visit.
In the back bedroom of the Local Shop
David's flicking through comics. Gorged on
sweets and squirrel, he howls for a mate.
Evenings find Chinnery and Briss at the Mason's Arms
propping up the bar, fingers sticky from their trades.
This is their town; they want no trouble here.

The Palace Pictures is no palace but the teens pile in,
counting the days till they can get away, from parents
intoning *in this house*, all rules and jangling keys.
What's all this shouting? More strangers will come.
New Road. The Local Shop will soon be an Asda,
the Palace a bingo hall. There will be no going back.

Jack Woolley's Dream   Tony Williams
i.m. Arnold Peters

In bed he listens to the radio:
the sound effects of Schmallenberg and five-bar gates,
unscripted chatter in The Bull.
Thou art a veal calf in the cellar's dark.
Thou art thy spouse's cousin. Glasses please.

Faceless Kareninas frolic naked there
with moody Grundys in the barn of the ear,
the boring county of all day in bed,
too sick to read. No one can visit now.
What keeps it closed is how the valleys lie

and roads drift off in silent snow to choke
the afternoon as with a maypole ribbon.
All this is the invention of a mind
which needs a playground for its childhood:
he in Grey Gables dreams Grey Gables real.

The town is thirsty for a dearth of time
and static's lull. There are antiques sobbing.
Tom's new sausage vies with burning Grace.
It is the vale of lengthening shadow, the bridge
which takes each soul beyond its Am.

Sisters   Tracey Herd

Dr. When am I most real?
—Virginia Stuart Cunningham, *The Snake Pit*

Atlanta burned down months before you fled the scene,
Safely captured on celluloid, the city façade that never was.
You were half dead from giving birth. Strange how both sisters
Fled the flames in their most famous films and how Melanie
    loved Scarlett
Like a sister. Rhett told Scarlett harshly: *She loves you, let that*
    be your curse.
In the back of the wagon you showed tenderness, not fear as you
    reached out weak arms
For the son who almost killed you. Then the pain. You couldn't
    even twist
Your gold wedding band for comfort as you'd given it away for
    the cause.
You had so little left but courage. You were the only one of the
    four main leads
Who died on celluloid. Now you have outlived them all by
    decades, your quiet strength
You were the only actress who wanted Melanie, seeing in her
    qualities
That most were blind to. *I loved her so. Melanie was…a caring*
    person.
A good woman but also an intelligent woman and a tough woman.
Most
Of all she was a…woman with a great capacity for happiness.

Perhaps, in the world of the screen, you connect with your sister
    or do
You simply not bother to watch each other? Do certain lines
    make you cry
Or smile. *There's a naturally strong rivalry between sisters*
    (Dark Mirror)
Two twins, one good, the other evil. You played them both. So
    who was real:

The nervous, loving one, the knife-wielding lunatic who played
     a symphony
on her sister's nerves? The good twin believed her sister innocent.
She started jumping at shadows, swallowing sleeping pills then
     waking at the brief,
 bright light which swept the bedroom and then was gone when
     she awoke.
But it was The Snake Pit where I think you almost touched, in
     the asylum
Where you cast off your name, your husband and your own
     beauty.
Zipped up to the chin in the ice bath, you had visions of the
     stormy
Waters off Manderley. But only briefly. I wanted to create a rose,
a hybrid to bring you both together. But that would be too
     elaborate.
You were both blue girls with golden hope, apart. I picked your
     flower,
The name almost an afterthought. Forget-me-not.

Joan Fontaine and Rebecca   Tracey Herd

You were never given a name of your own. The dead had a name,
Rebecca, and the sad lunatic down at the shack by the shore.
Even that damned house had a name: Manderley.
When you broke the porcelain figurine, I thought it was a portent
 Of things to come. I thought your fragile mind would shatter.
You were always huddled against the world, all nervous, flitting
     gestures.
Handing out the scripts, Hitchcock casually let slip that the cast
     and crew
Hated you. Olivier had no time for you. He wanted his Scarlett,
     black-haired

With eyes the colour of a dangerous green sea. He wanted to
    drown.
Her dark hair blowing in the wind… Who was Danvers really
    taunting you with?
You walked into the West Wing with its view of the sea. Danvers
    followed silently
To present Rebecca's wardrobe of fine, expensive things,
lingerie she held onto a little too long, a
monogrammed pillow slip , the nightgown by the
immaculately turned down bed as if each dawn
Rebecca would return from the tour of her domain and
slip silently into her gown. *Have you ever*
seen anything so delicate? Clumsily you turned and
ran from the room but you returned.
In Rebecca's cursed final masquerade costume, you leaned out
    into the misty night,
Mrs Danvers perched like an angel of death at your china white,
    flawless shoulder
Whispering as if from far far away, out at sea , luring the tiny
    vessel onto the rocks.
Rebecca echoes her entreaties from the ocean floor, coughing
    up rocks and shells.
She is possessed by Rebecca, her memory sailing at the edge of
    reason. Would you
Have jumped had the warning flares not shot up? I like to think
    not. You were
The only one of them with any sense. *She can't speak. She can't*
    bear witness.
She can't harm you any more. But nobody bothered to listen.
    Ship of fools.
In the end, it wasn't quite the burning of Atlanta, but Manderley
    put on
Quite a show, brutal against the dark skies, a false dawn and
    Mrs Danvers
Dancing dementedly like Rebecca's puppet for the last time,
    running
From window to window. And you, walking placidly with
    Rebecca's dog

Over the lawn in front of a burning skeleton. In the end, fragile
  girl with no name
Whose father painted the same tree for eternity, you survived
  them all.

Vertiginous   John Canfield

Madeleine

The swirl at the back of her hair is a vortex to fall
into. The red that flares about her face
is the blood that speeds its circuit in you.

When you save a life, the proverb says that you
become responsible, so fall
for her, let the swell consume you both. Face

it Scottie, you're in love with a ghost, a face
from a dream, and when she climbs where you
cannot follow you will watch her fall.

Another fall, another face to centrifugally haunt you.

Judy

Seek her, see her, follow her, call
on her, take her out to the same red place,
dress her, light her, until you can see right through

her. She'll plead, but convince her to see it through,
it can't matter to her at all if you call
her by someone else's name. Be sure to place

her in the same posed position when back at her place
and the neon charge will run through
you. Can you live with a ghost Scottie? It's your call.

Desire calls you back to a place that is not through with you.

The 39 Steps   Richard Watt

Once a railroad sleeper,
Hannay was frightfully sorry to flee
for the Scotch hinterland
but for his quarry, a new world
opened bright and skewbald.

Am I right, sir?

The ruler of a foreign power
hooked you from off stage
to hurtle over hills and level crossings,
into kailyards and bothies un-capital.

Scrabble pell-mell for Mackintoshes, MacGuffins—
a device that renders the engine sound—
careering through the ribs
of a mad, glinting giant.

Have you heard the one about—chocolate, cigarettes—
he's a madman—standard whalebone—I'll be right along.

Pamela came on at Killin,
flushed from the exchange
pistons ground the ballast at the pull cord's press
as our vista, shared unwitting, slowed.

Am I right, sir?

You then flitted as an archer
who, at every inn ate food meant for someone else
ran from a hostile house
and slept with microfiche.

Peter O'Toole Teaches The Last Emperor Some Yeats Dawn Wood

though it is said
you'll never leave the palace
until the great tree falls
in a great wind,
until the monkeys scatter
to the corners of the earth—
then the Son of Heaven,
the Lord of Ten Thousand Years,
will ride again the dragon—

this enterprise—
that you, yourself, are barely there,
that the whole forest is overcome
and none of the cities are forbidden—
ten thousand years of clearings
wrought to counterpoint
and never will your clothing
weave so eloquent a coat.

Marathon Man   Fiona Ritchie Walker

Her gran says
he never used his titles
though he deserved them all,
that her best Friday nights
were with her sisters
in the picture palace stalls,
gazing into his black and white eyes,
their painted mouths pouting
at the tilt of his Romeo bow.

Her gran says
he only answered to Larry,
which is why she chose the name,
ending up with Laura
when none of them were boys.
Now every birthday
the family replace more videos with DVDs,
though she's no time for Colin Firth.
Larry's the best Darcy of them all.

Her gran says
he ruined it in 1976,
there she was with a bag of toffees
in a top price row
when he came on the screen,
torturing that nice lad from *The Graduate*,
and all in colour too.
No wonder she couldn't face a second sweet,
her gums aching all the way home.

Please Be Dan Dare!   Tom Kelly

Ken, you might not like his conservative (with a small c) outlook,
his body language may change
watching your films but (for one production only)
can you wear his hat and take control,
save a million unemployed kids,
steer the craft, be Dan Dare and take Digby from Wigan
to something better than this?

So Ken, before you squint through the camera lens,
please take up Dan's mantle, if only for me,
aged seven-and-three-quarters in Jarrow,
think Billy Casper without the kestrel,
afraid of the dark and Tories me and me da hated.
Please save us
from these posh boys that make me so angry I have to lose myself
in Frank Hampson's drawings of Dan leading his crew
against the Mekon: we need you to be Dan Dare,
'Quiet, please. Roll camera. Action.'

Samurai   Crista Ermiya

*'When men don't trust each other, it makes
the world a hell'*[1]

In the village, samurai and bandit
are two words for one idea.
Mirror selves battle
across a mudscape of farmers,
livestock, rice and despair.
They are wolves sloping down hills,
over bridges and plains to their prey.
They are wolves in villagers' clothing,
building walls in defence of the fearful.
This is a war of attrition.
At the foothills of his companions' graves,
Takashi Shimura intones
'We are the losers, yet again.'[2]
Today, a soldier is hacked to death
in a street in London.
A terrorist apologises to the women;
in another circumstance he would help
carry their prams and their children.
His hands are gloves
of the very deepest red.

[1]Rashomon
[2]The Seven Samurai

A Spark   Degna Stone
i.m. Kenneth Arrowsmith Stone

...and it's like I'm floating
with the weight of the universe pressing
against every part of my body

and I long for the peace of an abandoned city
piled high with cubes of compressed rubbish
and the barest hint that human life could return...

I want to transform into an angular robot
with a naïve understanding of life and love,
who prefers the magic of a Zippo lighter to the fire

of a diamond ring; who follows his love across
the universe, recharges in the glare of the sun,
not needing to breathe—

Instead, on Earth, it feels like we've forgotten how to dance.
Your writing jitters like you'd been caught in a sandstorm—
'I think I am becoming unwell...'

We keep our heads down, remember the days
when blue skies were animated
with cartoon-perfect clouds

forget that we haven't learned to repair ourselves
and no spark of electricity
can bring you back to who you were.

Renga! A Dialogue Between Worlds?
Kirsten Irving & Jon Stone

Jubei! You bastard.
Come out so I can season
you with gunpowder.

> *Kuchiki! At the Shiba shack!*
> *Had I both arms I'd choke you.*

Dammit, Megumi,
you can't talk to me like that—
and put some clothes on!

> *Soul, my little scythey boy!*
> *What's with the nosebleed, Cool Guy?*

Cool Guy?! So, Lisker,
you're behind this! You and your
hyper-Zoanoids!

> *We're all one, Major. Petals*
> *in the rapids. Let us merge.*

You don't get it, Ken.
I'm nothing like you! In fact,
you're already dead.

> *You can't stand it, Kaneda.*
> *Being the weak one. Hurts, yeah?*

P & P   Eleanor Livingstone

Wholesome enough as background viewing
for Saturday teatime and Arthur Montford
with the football results—*Forfar 4, East Fife 5*—
their speeded up cover versions of Beatles' songs

squealed all the way home and encouraged us
to play 45 rpm singles at 78. That one wore red
and one wore blue went largely unnoticed
in a childhood where so much was black and white.

Looking back, our growing up from start to finish
flashed by in light years, flew across the universe
so we could reach the moon and walk on it perhaps,
with Pinky and Perky together showing us the way.

Quantum entanglement   Pippa Goldschmidt

In 1927 Laurel and Hardy
investigate the nature of reality
while Einstein and Bohr
form their double act.

Laurel wears a bowtie
Einstein wears a necktie
Hardy wears a necktie
and Bohr wears a bowtie.

Made of particles they don't yet understand
they're propagating through the future
coming soon to a screen near you.

Tell me that again, says Einstein
Bohr mugs at the camera—
If you watch two particles A and B,
and measure the momentum of A
he fiddles with his bowtie—
the momentum of B is known.

Tell me that again, says Einstein.
It's spooky action at a distance, says Laurel
Now that makes sense, says Hardy.

When Laurel cries
when Hardy grins
when Einstein sticks his tongue out
we laugh.

Everything's connected, says Bohr
you can't separate us
we're LaurelandHardy.

The Love that Runs Backwards   Matthew Griffiths

I never writ, nor no man ever loved
Who didn't dick about in Eden after dark.
If this be error and upon me proved,
I failed the poem that had me by heart
But beats it out even to the edge of doom.
She has my measure, I am twice her groom.

Love alters not with his brief hours and weeks
In which we're shooting *Woolf* but Nicholls seeks
Within his bending sickle's compass come-
Hither/Go-to-hell looks nursed at home.
Love's not Time's fool, though rosy lips and cheeks
Are more forgivingly filmed in monochrome.

Whose worth's unknown, although his height be taken
When she plays focus to the camera's arc?
It is the star to every wandering bark
I make my lines into. My passion's waking,
That looks on tempests and is never shaken
And stays the flint on which she strikes her spark.
O no, it is an ever-fixèd mark,
This mask, that moulds the man I have forsaken

Or bends with the remover to remove,
Hands cupped. Delivering each of these lines,
Which alters when it alteration finds,
I near the start, and words that come above
Admit impediments. Love is not love.
I am not Richard Burton, even re-signed,
Let me not to the marriage of true minds.

Never Forget   Kathleen Kenny
i.m. Eleanor Whinn-O'Shea

You received the box set
and my note about memories:
you and your friends
riding the ranges of Chapel House
like Liz in National Velvet,
Grand National winning jockeys.

After heavy days of chemo bags
you open a DVD
take a shot of onscreen steam:
Cat on a Hot Tin Roof,
Liz raising a thick dark eyebrow
over a flash of violet blue.

Later, high on her throne, Cleopatra
is borne into Rome to meet her true love.
She lowers a frill of double lashes
beauty and pain instilled
you drop your head of summer red
thirty years old, but only four days left.

No time for gowns in the Final Act.
Instead of wedding white you wear
a favoured purple dress, are carried
through The Christie on a bridal bed,
all morphine fix and newly married bliss
and never to meet with middle age,

see the Burtons stage
Who's Afraid of Virginia Woolf.
Look, there is your groom in the cold chapel
still crying to Take That: *And we're still so young,
and we hope for more. But remember this,
we are not invincible. We are only people.*

King Leer   Rachel McCrum

In the beginning
there was cutie fare
And cutie fare begat groovy fare
And cutie fare begat groovy fare begat nudie fare
And cutie begat groovy begat nudie
begat but it's just entertainment dear
begat but baby this is satire
begat pleading the First Amendment, sir
begat fantasy begat fixation begat obsession begat frustration
    begat frustration begat frustration begat
'Now lift that skirt, honey, just a little bit more. Lift it. Lift it.
    Lift it just a little bit more'.

In the beginning
Kitten Natividad is dancing like she's hurting
cantilevered tits teetering and the camera is a static, dribbling glare.

In the beginning,
King Leer is plastering over plotholes with a honky tonk
    soundtrack
and good ol Uncle Joe is telling you
that this is just soft sweet good ol fashioned fun fare
and cutie begat groovy begat nudie

begat this is where we are
begat lads mags at eye candy level
begat girls in tiny dresses and stripper shoes
not knowing if they're allowed to be proud
of their bodies
begat boys not knowing how to react to a woman's body
(begat boys not knowing what to do with a woman's body)
begat hardcore sex ed from gleaming mobile screens
and no one knowing that it's supposed to be something
you both enjoy
begat endless thinspo selfies of suckjob pouts because we all know

we look skinnier from down there
begat Saturday nights tilting at cobblestones to catcalls and
    packhowls
and someone, someone tell me that this is still just
just soft sweet good ol' fashioned fun fare
which it never was.
and cutie begat groovy begat nudie.

Two tit job time bombs later, Kitten Natividad still dances like
    she's hurting
and the old priapic Satyr still presides
King Leer
over his cutie groovy nudie fare.

PEDRO ALMODOVAR

Sheffield by Almodovar   Helen Mort

And we've been cast as villains overnight—
your silver trenchcoat, my unnecessary smile.
Cartoon pipettes have turned the foundries
yellow, crimson, blue. Our story happens
in reverse: the cars speed backwards
through Broomhill, a new rain levitates,
a needle drinks a misplaced inky heart.
I swallow everything I said, but just when we
run out of script there's always someone
with a mandolin, crooning below the plastics factory
so sweet the audience becomes a sigh.
And two frames after the epiphany, the tape
gets stuck. The evening stalls. In the pub
where it started, the drinkers freeze
mid-toast. I can't move my lips. I can't
take that look off your face.

Queensboro   Matthew Macdonald

Tell me the story of a city
but start it off with fireworks
with clarinets, jazz we can all enjoy
this city is better by night
tell me the story of a city in black and white
you know the importance of good shading
spotlights and blindsight
you told me they don't do it with mirrors
but with rivers and the moon
tell me a love story, without any love
and then tell me how you found it anyway
lingering in the air between us
like the breath taken just
before a punchline
you know better than anyone
speaking should be more than subtitles
tell me why you love me
or rather, tell me why you love this city
I know that the city is me as much as I am her
let me listen to Gershwin one more time
let me stand on the corner with you
acting like neither one of us wants to admit
that I'll never be able to look at a lobster
without laughing
or visit Coney Island without
remembering which one is your house
and you'll touch my arm, just enough
to cause a shadow underneath the skin
tell me a story in skyscrapers and bridges
tell it in shadows and whispers
in long tracking shots, lingering
trickles of laughter around the edges
tell me a love story without any love
tell me the story of a city

Dear Mr Guthrie   Josephine Dickinson

When all around the globe the peeps are cryin' revolution
and ornery folks are losin' out while racket boys rake it in,
Woody what message would you write in the holy ground?
Woody, would I could hear your voice again.

> Woody, what would you sing if you were here to sing?
> Woody, what would you do?
> I cain't hear you but I'm listenin' for your fiery voice,
>   yes I'm listenin'.

When veterans in their thousands comin' home are doin'
    themselves in
and untried men are dumped in jail and the key is thrown away,
Woody what would you do with your hoping machine?
Woody what would you say?

> Woody, what would you sing if you were here to sing?
> Woody, what would you do?
> I cain't see you but I'm watchin' for your burning bush,
>   yes I'm watchin'.

When all the globe is hottin' up and killer storms are hittin'
and all the bees are dyin' and all the whistleblowers on the run,
Woody what message would you write in the holy ground?
Woody, would I could hear your voice again.

> Woody, what would you sing if you were here to sing?
> Woody, what would you do?
> I cain't hear you but I'm listenin' for your fiery voice,
>   oh I'm listenin'.

Come Dine With Me   Alistair Robinson

Come Dine With Me is not
about competitive cooking. It's
about God. It confirms that he is invisible
but all-seeing and, as I suspected, very
sarky. He is not a patient god. He is not a tolerant
god. He sees the faults in our little plans,
our ill-thought-out itineraries and, most of all,
our recipes. He does not hold back. He does not
hold his tongue. He makes jokes at our expense.
And he cracks them with other invisible, all-seeing
beings.

Come Dine With Me confirms a lot of the stuff in
the Bible. He meant that bit about Pride.
If we find our little jokes amusing, or we think our
decor is cool, he will smite us without mercy. He is
also cuttingly disdainful of those who think
great riches will inevitably be theirs. Much
of the New Testament material is, however, revealed to be
wishful thinking. God is particularly down on the meek,
and the naff (although the latter are not specified in
traditional versions of the Beatitudes).

Come Dine With Me is not
about competitive cooking. It
just looks like it is. That's the clever
thing. If it was billed as a programme about
religion, we'd switch over to watch a
crappy reality show instead.

The Boardroom   Paul Stephenson

I've godda tell ya. You're fired!
I don't like cheats. You're fired!
I don't like bottlers. You're fired!
I don't like upstarts. You're fired!
I don't like shirkers. You're fired!
I don't like wafflers. You're fired!
I don't like grassers. You're fired!
I don't like airheads. You're fired!
I don't like copycats. You're fired!
I don't like tell-tales. You're fired!
I don't like braggers. You're fired!
I don't like chancers. You're fired!
I don't like doormats. You're fired!
I don't like layabouts. You're fired!
I don't like cry-babies. You're fired!
I don't like piss-takers. You're fired!
I don't like bullshitters. You're fired!
I don't like smart alecs. You're fired!
I don't like shit-stirrers. You're fired!
I don't like arse-lickers. You're fired!
I don't like numbskulls. You're fired!
I don't like schmoozers. You're fired!
I don't like know-it-alls. You're fired!
I don't like free-loaders. You're fired!
I don't like lightweights. You're fired!
I don't like time-wasters. You're fired!
I don't like back-stabbers. You're fired!
I don't like motor-mouths. You're fired!
I don't like gossipmongers. You're fired!
I don't like social climbers. You're fired!
I don't like Hooray Henries. You're fired!
I don't like Moaning Minnies. You're fired!
I like poets. I've godda tell ya. You're hired!

The Sun   Dorothy Lawrenson

OUR BRAVE BOYS are all in caps, **Wills and Kate** are bold;
but Harry's front page news again,
been filmed with fags and booze again,
see EXCLUSIVE grainy photos of the Royal lad's night out.
Page 2 pits hate preachers against Justin Bieber
for seats on the first plane back home.
Xenophobic, moi? On the facing page
today's *intelligent, vibrant young woman*
is Bekki, 19, from Croydon.
Bekki agrees with Bertrand Russell that *it is not by delusion,*
however exalted, that mankind can prosper,
but only by unswerving courage in the pursuit of truth.
Phew, what a scorcher.
The centre pages swarm with celebs alive and dead:
Jacko, J-Lo, Jedward, to send us Mystic Meg-ward,
but not without some homespun, no-nonsense advice.
LOVE RAT HUBBY WANTS TO LEAVE ME:
Dear Deidre,
I love my man, I don't want him to go, though he's never treated me
   right;
he got three bridesmaids pregnant on our wedding night.
He knocks me about, says it's my fault he's still on the dole and the
   smack;
I don't want to lose him, Deidre! Oh how can I win him back?
Deidre can extricate anyone from a complex situation
(especially that three-in-a-bed romp
detailed for readers' delectation).
Who buys the paper calls the tune,
and seven million interested public can't be wrong.
They shall know the truth, and the truth costs 40p.
News of the *world*? Aim higher—this universe is heliocentric.
Hot off the press, or wrapping tomorrow's chips,
IT'S THE SUN WOT WON IT.

You're Jody Porter

warlike, happiest in the gutter,
a stack of bile barely masked with lavender,
punching at the bloodied and the already winded.
You're a fork-tongued apologist for CCTV,
a way to spend a thoughtless morning,
a wretched bundle of crooked tea.
You're the glossy pomp of failing states,
the fawning rag of Gog and Magog,
a baroque contrivance of stagecraft and hate.
You're an anti-paper, a hatchet job.
A carapace protecting the few from the mob.
The schoolchum of fracking and Thatcher the Great.
The bludgeon of democracy, a slouchy dog.
The scapegoater prince and blinder of sight.
The defender of all that is *good* and *noble* and *right*.

The Story of Dalston   Tim Wells

Newton Dunbar ran the Four Aces,
a pioneering club in Dalston;
not in the West End *fasharn* sense
but in real people's music sense—
reggae, soul, lovers, rave from the 60s,
the Four Aces was home to them all.

When Hackney Council knocked down
his club, developers built plush flats
next to the tube station
the Council had been promising us
since 1975—
the kind no-one local can afford.

Newton was asked
what's on the site of his club now?
Kissing his teeth in that Dalston way of old,
'Dem name a block after me' he conceded.
And how do you feel about that?
'One day it will be knocked down.'

God is a DJ   Valerie Laws
—Armin van Buuren, A State Of Trance @ Privilege, Ibiza,
    July 2013

No longer secret but still a cult, we faithful mass together
In a dark cathedral of ice, fire, lasers, glitter, acrobats
Instead of architecture. We dance with our arms reaching
Beyond the lofty roof, in heaven but still aspiring higher,
Our hands pulled up by music, in a State of Trance.
Thousands of us, blissful, euphoric, lifted above ourselves,
Full of love for each other and for Armin. Even his name
Almost a prayer, our smiling deity raises his own arms wide
In benediction. We feel right through us the soaring, building
Heartbeat of House, the waiting, waiting for the tune to break—
The ecstasy of release, the glorious electronic chords,
The flowing, intertwining riffs, the voices pure, angelic.

We are happy.

This is the blessing of religion, without the thou shalt nots,
The hate, the torture, oppression, hypocrisy, war.
Yet this is what was driven underground when ravers met
In empty factories gifted, ironically, by Thatcher the antichrist.
Persecuted by the law, they spread the Word through holy texts,
Driven to party at the extremes of the M25. Pleasure's a threat
To governments. But why? Why do they all adopt the dark side
Of religion, instead of this pure joy? Tonight if god is love,
God is a DJ, one of many, and we are one, the Privileged,
Our fingers stretched to touch Ibiza's stars, feel them tingle
Like frosty glitter against our skin. Our faces upturned
To receive the host's communion, chanting our responses
We are grateful not humble, all of us raised up, equally high.

'God is a DJ': trance track from the album Sunday 8PM by
Faithless, 1998

Up! Agnes Marton

Here I am, the Red Stormshaper!
I scream to tame
and whisper to make you summersault with me,
skip up, up, UP!

Drown your voice
in feral fairy tales, a hoarse feast.
Then join in neverhome arias,
searching.

Here I am, pig-tailed witch
of wolf-charming spells and hopscotch,
here I am, flying, Odin's eight-legged horse.

I'm Diva Polihoppp.

I'm Demon Lollipop.

Skip!
Trust the arcs between the joints.

Give names to your kites and skyrockets
after places like Wirrabilla, it means Devil Fish.

Joy, no end. Skip. Shiver.

What I was doing when the house caught fire   Lisa Matthews

attic window catches sunrise, opens to let all light in and lost birds out—the hand that pushes the catch has not slept, it has forgotten the push and pull of it, the breath and breathing, the wreath and writhing, the smooth and sheath of familial grooves cut cold into peat—in the scullery, mother shouts to *turn it down* but the striking hooves drown her out—then the helicopters come and my lifejacket is ripped from my neck—climbers search their way up the backyard trellis, the cotton wool thud of the wrecking ball so many streets away and getting closer—lyrics like swallows, like bombs, or even donkeys if you please—love walking away, in the dark, in Baghdad, in Romanian folksong, on deserted platforms, in quiet wombs and dirty rooms—the indefinite article—Mrs Houdini passing it, first with one sorry kiss then another; words in mouths, on bitten lips, under the enamel of our teeth

this is what creation sounds like, its shadow slouch and slant across the living room floor, its stain blooming above the mantle as it shudders into corners hardly speaking at all; and it crawls deep down inside me, and there it rests with the wood grain and the pointing in the wall, and there it has settled and it will form, and it will form, and it will form—another attic window no doubt catches sunset, letting lost birds in, and all the light out

Strictly for Men   Tim Turnbull

Rolls his eyes, gives conspiratorial half smile,
but no, young man, no you don't
recruit me so easily to your bullshit ideological
bullshit, wherein real men don't dance but
stand awkwardly at party fringes slurping sour
pints in begrudged best togs, bought by mummy-
substitute wives and girlfriends goes without
saying, dahling; no, no, no, au contraire,
mon cher—and yes, that's French, and no, I don't
share your witless panto-detestation of all things
continental—for what you would see of a Saturday
evening, in the unlikely event that you could pay
attention without exercising your already over-
exercised jaw for more than fifteen seconds, is
people learning, despite their best efforts at
self-enscupperment, not merely to do the footwork,
perfect, within reasonable bodily limitations,
carriage and posture, but to love—that's L-O-V-E,
as in abandon selfhood unto—the dahnce.
And the tragedy for you, old sausage, is not that,
with a smidge of effort, you could not manage it,
but that you can't even make your piddling, hidebound
brain imagine dancing the Argentine tango with
Flavia Cacace. Here, however, muttonhead,
is a prescription, a starter on the road to recovery,
viz. a three-point manifesto for a new model
of masculinity—commit to memory and recite
daily by way of a mantra:

1.   Cultivate elegance in dress and bearing.

2.   Never start a fight you are certain to win.

3.   Dance as if everyone was watching.

X Factor Maggie Doyle

His friends assured him he could sing,
had perfect pitch and everything.
They told him he could have it all,
send off the form, await the call.

His look was street, but stylised,
with tweedy cap and contact eyes.
They egged him on and praised his style
and he believed them, for a while.

Then, after queuing for an age
he stepped onto the lonely stage.
He couldn't see the faceless crowd,
but knew his voice would make them proud.

He hit them with his finest work,
but didn't see the people smirk.
Stifled laughter, eyebrows raised
went unnoticed, he unfazed.

The judges did not treat him well;
they said his look would never sell;
his voice was awful, like his song,
and they were rarely ever wrong.

He left the stage with eyes downcast
but understood the game at last;
some acts become the golden calf
while others serve to make us laugh.

Wrap   Andy Jackson

In the vaults below the studio are shelves of film,
festering in cans by night, sweating silver nitrate
till they separate into a slurry and a whiff of vinegar.

Long ago I must have breathed those wind-borne flakes
of celluloid, accumulating as a dark infection in my lungs,
spreading like a virus to my blood, my nerves, my brain,

until the fragments of the images they once contained
became the pictures of my thoughts. These days
the world seems undercranked, my memories of its

opening scenes as faded as an ageing negative, although
tomorrow always has its possibilities, an unread script
in a sealed envelope, a reel of unexposed stock.

There are whispers of a sequel, prequel, threequel,
but the final scene is in the can; *wind, reel and print.*
Until we meet again, here's to you, my cast and crew.

Notes on Contributors

Tiffany Atkinson's third collection, *So Many Moving Parts*, was published by Bloodaxe in 2014 and she is currently working on a new collection exploring health and illness. She is Professor of Poetry at the University of East Anglia.

Janette Ayachi was born in 1982 and graduated from Edinburgh University with an MSc in Creative Writing; she has published in over fifty international journals and anthologies and is the author of poetry collections *Pauses at Zebra Crossings* and *A Choir of Ghosts*. She likes whiskey and wild women.

Ruth Aylett teaches computing at Heriot-Watt University, wonders why we let the world go on as it does, and feels compelled to write poems and short stories. She has been published by Red Squirrel Press, *Poetry Scotland, Textualities, New Writing Scotland,* Doire Press, *Ink, Sweat and Tears,* and others. More at www.macs.hw.ac.uk/~ruth/writing.html.

Simon Barraclough is the author of the Forward-finalist debut, *Los Alamos Mon Amour* (Salt, 2008), *Bonjour Tetris* (Penned in the Margins, 2010) and *Neptune Blue* (Salt, 2011). He is the editor of *Psycho Poetica* (Sidekick Books, 2012) and co-author of *The Debris Field* (Sidekick Books, 2013). He is currently poet in residence at the Mullard Space Science Laboratory.

Bob Beagrie lives in Middlesbrough and is a Senior Lecturer in Creative Writing at Teesside University. Collections include *Yoik*, (Cinnamon Press 2008), *The Seer Sung Husband,* (Smokestack Books, 2010) *Glass Characters* (Red Squirrel Press 2011).

Jo Bell is a poet whose work has won the Charles Causley Prize and been twice nominated for a Ted Hughes Award. She is the Canal Poet Laureate for the UK. Her collection *Kith* is available from Nine Arches in spring 2015.

Dzifa Benson is a live artist and writer of prose, poetry, journalism and drama. She has read and performed at the London

Literature Festival and Glastonbury Festival. She was a writer-in-residence at the Courtauld Institute of Art from 2008 to 2009 and has also been widely published in anthologies, newspapers and magazines.

Anne Berkeley's pamphlet *The buoyancy aid and other poems* (Flarestack, 1997) sank without trace. She attained brief transatlantic notoriety with *The Joy of Six*. *The Men From Praga* (Salt, 2009) was shortlisted for the Seamus Heaney Centre first collection prize.

Julie Boden has been Poet in Residence at Symphony Hall, Birmingham since 2005 and BAFTA nominated in 2012. She writes poetry for page, stage and film. *Poetry and Piano* (with Steve Tromans) and her third play, *Cracked* (co-written with Mike Kenny) begin touring in 2014/15.

Cathy Bryant has won ten literary awards, including the Bulwer-Lytton Fiction Prize. She co-edited *Best of Manchester Poets* vols. 1–3, and her latest solo collection, *Look at All the Women*, was published by Mother's Milk Books in 2014.

Alan Buckley's pamphlet *Shiver* (tall-lighthouse) was a Poetry Book Society Choice. He works in Oxford as a psychotherapist, and as a school writer-in-residence for the charity First Story.

Mark Burnhope was born in 1982 and lives in Boscombe, Dorset. Mark's published work includes two chapbooks: *The Snowboy* (Salt, 2011) and *Lever Arch* (Knives Forks and Spoons Press, 2013), and a debut full collection: *Species* (Nine Arches Press, 2014).

Kevin Cadwallender is still a poet despite what he has sewn on the inside of his shirt. He is the author of numerous collections, including *Dances With Vowels* (Smokestack, 2009) and *Sagrada Familia* (Red Squirrel Press, 2010).

Robin Cairns has been described as 'A force of nature' by *Poetry Scotland* and 'Fall-off-the-couch funny' by the Edinburgh Guide.

Seasoned slammer and performer, his published works include *The Last Man With Sky* (Red Squirrel Press, 2008) and *Old Lochgelly* (Silkscreen Press).

Hazel Buchan Cameron is author of five poetry pamphlets including *The Currying Shop* (2007), which was joint winner of the Callum Macdonald Memorial Award in 2008. Red Squirrel Press published her collection *Finding IKEA* (2010). She is currently Writer in Residence for the Royal Scottish Geographic Society.

John Canfield grew up in Cornwall and now lives in London. His poems have appeared in various magazines and anthologies. He trained as an actor, but due to a clerical error currently works in an accounts department.

Jim Carruth has published six acclaimed poetry chapbooks. He has won the James McCash poetry competition and the McLellan Poetry Prize and been awarded a Robert Louis Stevenson Fellowship. Recently he edited an anthology of poetry for the Commonwealth Games and had his words etched in stone as part of Andy Scott's Kelpies project. In July 2014 Jim was appointed as Poet Laureate of Glasgow.

John Challis is a Creative Writing PhD candidate at Newcastle University, and in 2012 won a Northern Promise Award from *New Writing North*. His poems have appeared in magazines including *Clinic II, Iota, Magma* and *The Rialto*.

Daniel Cockrill's words have appeared in books, on stage, fridges, gallery walls, radio and television. He is the Co-founder of Bang Said The Gun and Page Match and is published by Burning Eye.

Anne Connolly is Irish and enjoys performing her poetry which often engages with the complexity of the country and its people. Her pamphlets are *Downside Up* and *Not entirely beautiful*. *Love-in-a-mist* is a Red Squirrel Press collection.

Tony Curtis was born in Dublin in 1955. Has written several books of poetry, most recently *Folk* (Arc publications, 2011) Pony (Occasional Press, 2013). He is currently working on a new collection for Arc Publications. He has been awarded The National Poetry Prize and is a member of *Aosdana*.

Jan Dean is a poet-in-schools and runs workshops for children and adults in libraries and at festivals. *The Penguin in Lost Property* (Macmillan) is her latest children's collection co-authored with Roger Stevens. www.jandean.co.uk

Josephine Dickinson has published four poetry collections, *Scarberry Hill* (The Rialto, 2001), *The Voice* (Flambard, 2004), *Silence Fell* (Houghton Mifflin Harcourt, 2007), and *Night Journey* (Flambard, November 2008). Current projects include a fifth poetry collection and a memoir, *The Leech Gatherer*.

Isobel Dixon's recent collections are *A Fold in the Map* and *The Tempest Prognosticator*. She loves cinema and thinks classic musicals should be prescribed on the NHS. www.isobeldixon.com.

Morgan Downie is an inveterate film watcher. He also writes short stories and poetry. His contribution to the world of celluloid comprises of an ongoing fictitious life of Ingmar Bergman. Any representation of actual character is purely coincidental.

Maggie Doyle was the First female Worcestershire Poet Laureate in 2012, director of the Worcestershire LitFest & Fringe; a quarter of the Decadent Poetry Divas and a founder member of Write Down Speak Up.

Crista Ermiya grew up in London, of Filipino and Turkish-Cypriot heritage, and lives in Newcastle-upon-Tyne with her husband and son. Her first short story collection, *The Weather in Kansas*, is forthcoming from Red Squirrel Press.

Sally Evans' books of poetry include *The Bees, Poetic Adventures in Scotland, Bewick Walks to Scotland* and *The Honey Seller*. She edits the *Poetry Scotland* broadsheet and runs the Callander Poetry Weekend.

Andrew C Ferguson is a poet, musician and performer living in Fife, Scotland. He could never understand why Scooby-Doo and the others split up to search for the bad guys when it was clearly such a flawed strategy.

Martin Figura was recently described in a hospital referral letter (bad back) as 'a pleasant 56 year old gentleman'. He lives in Norwich with Helen Ivory and her dismembered dolls.

Andrew Fox was born in Bristol in 1953 and educated in Dundee. He was subsequently employed as a civil servant, teacher and curator until his retirement in 2012, and is co-author (with John Glenday) of the anthology *Darkness & Snowfall* (1989).

Annie Freud's first full collection was *The Best Man That Ever Was* (Picador) Her second collection, *The Mirabelles* (Picador 2010) was a Poetry Book Society Choice and was short listed for the T S Eliot Prize. Her third collection will be published in 2015. She is also an artist and runs a thriving poetry writing group, The Cattistock Poets, based in West Dorset.

Eddie Gibbons was born in Liverpool, when it was in Lancashire. He currently lives in Aberdeenshire. *A Twist of Lime Street: New and Selected Poems* was published by Red Squirrel Press in 2013. He recently became a pensioner.

John Glenday's most recent collection, *Grain* (Picador 2009) was a Poetry Book Society Recommendation and shortlisted for the Ted Hughes Award and the Griffin Poetry Prize. His fourth collection is due for publication in 2015.

Pippa Goldschmidt's short stories, poetry and non-fiction have been making appearances for some time in various places including *Gutter, New Writing Scotland* and the *New York Times*.

Her novel *The Falling Sky* is published by Freight Books and her short story collection will be coming out in 2015.

Alison Grant is a graduate from the MLitt in Writing at Dundee University. In her day job she plans forests. Her writing has appeared in *New Writing Dundee, Gutter, New Writing Scotland* and various anthologies.

Matthew Griffiths has recently completed a PhD on modernist poetry and climate change, so by the time you read this, who knows what he'll be up to? His pamphlet, *How to be Late,* was published by Red Squirrel Press in 2013.

A.F. Harrold is a poet and performer who writes for children and adults. His poetry collections are published by Two Rivers Press and Burning Eye Books, and his children's novels are available from Bloomsbury. Find more at www.afharrold.com

Matt Harvey's books include *The Hole in the Sum of My Parts, Where Earwigs Dare* and *Mindless Body Spineless Mind.* He is the creator of Empath Man and Radio 4's Wondermentalist Cabaret. 'Fabulously understated' (*The Dorset Echo*).

John Hegley enjoyed Mr Magoo in his Luton childhood days, long before he had spectacles of his own. He was further educated in Bristol and at Bradford university, returning to his birthplace, London, where he lives alongside Dangercat, Ella.

W. N. Herbert is Professor of Poetry and Creative Writing at Newcastle University. He writes poetry and libretti, and is also an essayist, reviewer and translator. He is mostly published by Bloodaxe Books. Since 2013 he has also been the Dundee Makar.

Tracey Herd was born in Scotland and has lived there all her life. She has published two books of poetry with Bloodaxe and a third *Not in this World* is forthcoming in 2015. She has performed poetry readings in Russia and at Musselburgh racecourse.

Joan Hewitt lives in Tynemouth and was in her early sixties when her first collection Missing the Eclipse was published by Cinnamon Press in 2008. Now retired from university teaching, she has poems in several anthologies, including Northern Poetry Workshop's *In Your Own Time* (Shoestring).

Lindsey Holland is the founder of North West Poets. She's currently Poet in Residence at Chester Zoo. She's edited two anthologies and her collection *Particle Soup* appeared from The Knives Forks and Spoons Press in 2012.

Wayne Holloway-Smith's work has appeared in numerous journals and anthologies, most recently, *Oxford Poetry, Stop Sharpening Your Knives 5* and *Best British Poetry 2013*. In 2011, his debut pocketbook was published by Donut Press. He lives in London and is a Ph.D candidate at Brunel University.

Ric Hool has ten collections of published poetry. His work is featured in poetry magazines and journals in Europe, USA and UK. His *Selected Poems* (Red Squirrel Press, 2013) and *A Way of Falling Upwards* (Cinnamon Press, 2014) are recent titles.

Adam Horovitz was born in London but was brought up and now lives in Slad. He has published two pamphlets and a full collection of poetry, *Turning*, published by Headland in 2011. His book, *A Thousand Laurie Lees*, was published in June 2014.

Irene Hossack's poetry has been published internationally, most recently in *Gutter, Long Poem Magazine* and *Causeway/Cabhsair*. She was a mentee in the St. Mungo's Mirrorball Clydebuilt scheme and shortlisted for a New Writers Award 2010/11. She is a Lecturer in Creative Writing at the Open University.

Lesley Ingram was born in Yorkshire and lives in Ledbury. Her first poetry collection will be published by Cinnamon Press in 2015. She won the 2013 Ludlow Fringe Poetry competition, and has been published in various journals and anthologies.

Kirsten Irving is one half of the editorial team behind Sidekick Books. Her work has been translated into Russian and Spanish, shortlisted for the Forward and Bridport Prizes and thrown out of a helicopter. Her collection, *Never Never Never Come Back*, is available from Salt Publishing. Kirsten lives in London, where she works as a freelance copywriter.

Helen Ivory is a poet and artist. Her fourth collection is *Waiting for Bluebeard* (Bloodaxe). She is Course Director for the Continuing Education programme in Creative Writing for UEA/WCN and edits *Ink Sweat & Tears*.

Andy Jackson has edited several poetry anthologies including *Whaleback City* (with W. N. Herbert, Edinburgh University Press 2013), *Tour de Vers* (Red Squirrel Press, 2014) and *Split Screen*, the 2012 prequel to *Double Bill*. His solo collection *The Assassination Museum* (Red Squirrel Press, 2010) will be followed up by a second collection in 2015.

Lucy Jeynes is a poet who grew up in Yorkshire—the Jarvis Cocker, Arthur Scargill part, not the Brontes part. She is working on her first collection.

Joan Johnston teaches Creative Writing in Further Education and is currently a writer with elderly people in care. Widely published, her most recent collection, *The Daredevil: Scenes from a Bigamist Marriage* was published by Red Squirrel Press in 2011. She has a Hawthornden Fellowship and is working on her fifth collection.

Brian Johnstone has published six collections of poetry, most recently *Dry Stone Work* (Arc, 2014). His work appears on The Poetry Archive website. He has read at festivals from Macedonia to Nicaragua. brianjohnstonepoet.co.uk

Russell Jones is an Edinburgh-based writer and editor. He has a PhD in Creative Writing from Edinburgh University and has also published on the poetry of Edwin Morgan. www.poetrusselljones.blogspot.com.

Charlie Jordan is a radio presenter and a former Birmingham Poet Laureate; Charlie was 6ft tall aged just 12 but always had designs on Paisley Park from the top deck of the number 9 bus in Halesowen.

Tom Kelly was born in Jarrow and now lives further up the Tyne at Blaydon. He has had fifteen productions, plays and musicals, staged at the Customs House, South Shields. His seventh poetry collection, *I Know Their Footsteps*, was published by Red Squirrel Press in September 2013.

Will Kemp won the Envoi International and Debut Collection Award in 2010, and was second in the Keats-Shelley Prize 2013. His collections *Nocturnes* (2011) and *Lowland* (2013) were published by Cinnamon, as will his third, *The Painters Who Studied Clouds* (2015). www.wkemp.com.

Luke Kennard is the author of four volumes of poetry, the most recent being *A Lost Expression* (Salt, 2012). He lectures at the University of Birmingham.

Kathleen Kenny lives and writes in Newcastle. She has several published poetry collections to her credit, her most recent collection, *Travelling Like Eggs* was published by Red Squirrel Press in 2011. Currently she is busy revising and editing her much anticipated autobiographical novel: *The Satellites of Jupiter*, due from Red Squirrel Press in 2015.

Dorothy Lawrenson was born in Dundee, and studied Fine Art at the University of Edinburgh. She is editor of the award-winning Perjink Press, and her own poetry is published in the chapbooks *Under the Threshold* and *The Year*. She is currently undertaking an MFA in Poetry at Texas State University.

Valerie Laws is a poet, performer, crime novelist, playwright, sci-art installation specialist and mathematician/physicist, with thirteen books published. World-infamous for spray-painting poetry on sheep, she works with pathologists, neuroscientists and anatomists. www.valerielaws.com.

Ira Lightman is a poet, author of 3 books and several chapbooks. In his double column poems (Trancelated at www.ubu.com/ubu) he employs quoted text and translations in collages. He makes public art, organizing a community's poems into visual art. He broadcasts on BBC Radio 3's *The Verb*. He has set Creeley, Gunn and Sward etc. to ukulele.

Jack Little was born in 1987 and is a young British poet, translator and editor based in Mexico City. He is the founder of The Ofi Press. www.ofipress.com.

Pippa Little lives in Northumberland. *Overwintering* (Carcanet) came out in 2012 and was shortlisted for The Seamus Heaney Centre Prize. She is currently working on a commission for the Bloodaxe Poetics of the Archive project.

Eleanor Livingstone is a poet (*Even the Sea,* Red Squirrel Press, 2010, was shortlisted for the London New Poetry award for first collections), editor (*Skein of Geese* and *Migraasje*) and Director of the *StAnza* festival www.stanzapoetry.org.

Chris McCabe has published three collections of poetry and a number of collaborations, including *Pharmapoetica*, which was shortlisted for the 2014 Ted Hughes Award. In the Catacombs has just appeared with Penned in the Margins who will publish his next collection in December.

Rachel McCrum is originally from a small seaside town in Donaghadee, now in Edinburgh, via Oxford, New Zealand and Manchester. Her first pamphlet *The Glassblower Dances* won the 2012 Callum MacDonald Award. She is the Broad part of Rally & Broad, Edinburgh's cabaret of words, music and lyrical delight.

Matthew Macdonald writes about a great many things, and the excuse to write about Woody Allen was too much to ignore. His pamphlet, *Who Are Your People?* was published in July 2014. He blogs at mattmacdonaldpoetry.wordpress.com, and watches too much TV too much of the time.

Paul McGrane is the co-founder of Forest Poets in Walthamstow, co-editor of *Nutshell Magazine,* and the only Poetry Society Membership Manager. Poems recently published in *The Poetry of Sex* (Penguin), and *The Interpreters House.*

McGuire is a thin Glaswegian poet of frank and direct disposition. Published *Riddled With Errors* Clydesidepress (2005). Red Squirrel Press: *Everybody lie down and no one gets hurt* (2013) and *As I sit quietly, I begin to smell burning* (2014).

Rob A. Mackenzie is reviews editor for *Magma* Poetry magazine and his most recent poetry collection is *The Good News* (Salt 2013). He played guitar and saxophone for Glasgow art-pop band, *Pure Television.* Sad music makes him feel briefly optimistic.

Jane McKie's poetry collections include *Morocco Rococo* (Cinnamon, 2007), *When the Sun Turns Green* (Polygon, 2009), and the pamphlet *Garden of Bedsteads* (Mariscat, 2011). She teaches Creative Writing at the University of Edinburgh.

Andrew McMillan was born in South Yorkshire in 1988. His debut collection, *physical,* is forthcoming from Jonathan Cape. He currently lectures in Creative Writing at Liverpool John Moores University.

Ian McMillan is a prolific writer and broadcaster. He has published several collections of poetry, most recent of which are *This Lake Used to be Frozen: Lamps* (Smith/Doorstep, 2011) and *Talking Myself Home* (John Murray, 2008). He presents Radio 3's weekly spoken word show *The Verb* and is writer-in-residence for Barnsley FC.

Roy Marshall's first pamphlet was *Gopagilla* (2012) and a full collection of poems, *The Sun Bathers* was published by Shoestring Press in 2013. Roy lives and works in Leicestershire.

Agnes Marton is a Hungarian-born poet. Her most recent publications include *Penning Perfumes* and *Lines Underwater* in the

UK, and *Estuary: A Confluence of Art and Poetry*, *Drifting Down the Lane* and *Exquisite Duet* in the USA.

Lisa Matthews is a poet, collaborator, rhythm guitarist and all-round water and Kate Bush obsessive. She lives by the sea and is never more than thirty feet away from a source of music.

Helen Mort's first collection *Division Street* (Chatto & Windus) was published in 2013 and shortlisted for the Costa and T. S. Eliot prizes. She is the current Derbyshire Poet Laureate.

Niall O'Sullivan has published three poetry collections with Flipped Eye and teaches at London Metropolitan University. He runs Poetry Unplugged, a long running weekly open mic at Covent Garden's Poetry Cafe.

Ian Parks' collections include *Shell Island*, *Love Poems 1979–2009*, and *The Exile's House*. He was writer in residence a Gladstone's Library in 2012 and Writing Fellow at DMU Leicester from 2012 to 2014. *The Cavafy Variations* was a Poetry Book Society Choice.

Ellen Phethean's first collection *Breath* (Flambard Press, 2009, reprinted by Red Squirrel Press, 2014) was shortlisted for the London New Poetry Award 2010. Her second collection, *Portrait of the Quince as an Older Woman*, was published by Red Squirrel Press in 2014. www.diamondtwig.co.uk.

Andrew Philip's latest book of poetry, *The North End of the Possible*, was published by Salt in 2013. It followed his multi-award nominated debut collection, *The Ambulance Box* (Salt, 2009). His work has appeared in several anthologies, including *Split Screen*. He is currently poetry editor for Glasgow-based Freight Books and Scots language editor for *Irish Pages*.

Pauline Plummer has had three collections of poetry published, most recently *Bint* (Red Squirrel Press, 2011) and a verse novella *From Here to Timbuktu* (Smokestack 2012). In December 2014 a collection of her short stories will be published by Red Squirrel Press. She was a founding editor of Mudfog Press.

Porky the Poet, also known as Phill Jupitus, has been writing and performing poetry since 1983. His work has appeared in *The Guardian, Rising, The Morning Star* and *The Reader.* He performs regularly at the Edinburgh Fringe Festival and lives in Leigh-on-Sea.

Jody Porter is poetry editor of socialist daily newspaper *The Morning Star.* His work has appeared in *Magma, The Best British Poetry 2013, Poems in Which, Catechism: Poems for Pussy Riot* and elsewhere.

Creator and destroyer of the infamous Gingham Diva Chloe Poems, Gerry Potter is now on an intrepid mission to launch his genre-defying opus *The Chronicles of Folly Butler* onto the world, which is the fifth in a ten book series of life-story and imaginings.

Tom Pow's latest books are *A Wild Adventure—Thomas Watling, Dumfries Convict Artist* and *Concerning the Atlas of Scotland and other poems* (both Polygon). In 2003, he organised an exhibition with Hugh Bryden called *My Dad was a Cowboy.*

Sheenagh Pugh lives in Shetland. Her current collection is *Short Days, Long Shadows* (Seren 2014). She can quote Round the Horne far too extensively.

Angela Readman's poems have won the Mslexia Poetry Competition, and the Essex Poetry Prize. Her collection *Strip* was published by Salt. She also writes stories.

Heather Reid is originally from Lancashire but now lives near Perth. She writes poetry and short fiction, some of which has been published or broadcast on radio and some of which hasn't.

Carolyn Richardson is a Director of the Scottish Writers Centre, author, external examiner of creative writing programmes and an assiduous literary festival-goer. She is developing links and writing courses with Montolieu, a French National Booktown.

Chris Riley is a Bedford-based teacher and writer whose day job is in Krakow, Poland where she writes a regular column in the local ex-pat newspaper, *The Krakow Post*. She rarely buys insurance and almost never shops around.

Elizabeth Rimmer usually writes about rain, rivers, birds, landscape, and more rain. Her first collection *Wherever We Live Now* was published in 2011 by Red Squirrel Press, her second collection is forthcoming in September 2015.

Alistair Robinson, from South Shields, has had two collections published by Red Squirrel Press—*Stereograms of the Dead* in 2009 and *The Land Before Yoghurt* in 2014. He's also a journalism lecturer, media historian and jazz musician.

Nikki Robson enjoys capturing life in poetry and holds an MLitt in Writing Practice and Study from the University of Dundee. From Northern Ireland, she lives in Kirriemuir with her husband and 3 children.

Stevie Ronnie is a writer and artist. His first collection of poetry is *Manifestations* (Red Squirrel Press, 2013). Awards include: a Northern Promise Award, a MacDowell Fellowship, two GFA awards from Arts Council England and a Jerwood/Arvon menteeship.

Jacqueline Saphra's book, *The Kitchen of Lovely Contraptions* was nominated for the Aldeburgh First Collection Prize. An illustrated book of prose poems, *If I Lay on my Back I Saw Nothing but Naked Women*, is forthcoming from The Emma Press.

Josephine Scott was born in Northumberland and spent her childhood in Australia. She has an MA in Creative Writing and had her first collection, *Sparkle and Dance*, published by Red Squirrel Press in 2009. Her second collection, *Rituals*, is to be published by RSP in October 2014.

Michael Scott is from Swindon. He has been published by *The Morning Star, Ink Sweat and Tears, And Other Poems* and *The Interpreter's House*. Michael believes that the presence of a chimpanzee in any poem will enhance it.

Hilda Sheehan's first collection of poetry, *The Night My Sister Went to Hollywood*, is published by Cultured Llama (www.culturedllama.co.uk). A pamphlet, *Frances and Martine* is due out in September 2014 from Dancing Girl Press.

Nancy Somerville's work has appeared in various magazines and anthologies. Her poem 'The Big Hooley' was in *100 Favourite Scottish Poems* (Luath Press 2006). Her collection, *Waiting for Zebras* (Red Squirrel Press 2008), received the publisher's award in 2010. She is a member and former convenor of Edinburgh's Shore Poets: www.shorepoets.org.uk

Paul Stephenson recently completed the Jerwood/Arvon mentoring scheme and 'graduated' from the Poetry Business Sheffield Writing School. He won first prize in the South Bank Poetry Competition. His other poem about the Apprentice, which involves a lot of beetroot, was published in *Magma*. Paul is a university lecturer/researcher currently living in Paris.

Jim Stewart has published poems in various outlets over many years. He teaches Literature and also Creative Writing at the University of Dundee. He is a co-editor of Virginia Woolf's first novel in the forthcoming Cambridge University Press Edition.

Degna Stone is an award-winning poet and performer based in Northumberland. She is co-founder of *Butcher's Dog* poetry magazine and her second pamphlet *Record and Play* is published by Red Squirrel Press.

Jon Stone has published a full collection, *School of Forgery*, with Salt in 2012 and co-edited an anthology of computer game poetry, *Coin Opera 2* (Sidekick, 2013). His work has also featured in several anthologies, including *Where Rockets Burn Through*

(Penned in the Margins, 2012), *Drawn to Marvel* (Minor Arcana Press, 2014) and *Adventures in Form* (PitM, 2012). His website is at www.gojonstonego.com.

Judi Sutherland works in the pharmaceutical/biotech sector and also has an MA in Creative Writing from Royal Holloway, University of London. She has had poems published in *New Statesman, Acumen, Oxford Poetry* and *Ink, Sweat and Tears,* among others.

George Szirtes has published some fifteen books of poetry, most recently *New and Collected Poems* (2008), *The Burning of the Books* (2009) and *Bad Machine* (2013). He was awarded the T S Eliot Prize for *Reel* (2004).

Judith Taylor comes from Coupar Angus, but now she's written a poem about it she can't go back. She lives in Aberdeen and is the author of two pamphlet collections, *Earthlight* (Koo Press, 2006) and *Local Colour* (Calder Wood Press, 2010).

Sheila Templeton writes in both Scots and English. A winner in both the McCash Scots Language and the Robert McLellan poetry competitions, she was also Makar of the Federation of Writers Scotland 2009–2010. Her latest collections are *Digging for Light* (New Voices Press, 2011) and *Tender is the North* (Red Squirrel Press, 2013).

Jacqueline Thompson is a Creative Writing PhD student at The University of Edinburgh. Her poems have appeared in a range of publications including *New Writing Scotland, Gutter, For A' That* (Dundee University Press) and *The Scotsman.*

Angela Topping has published seven collections of poetry and three pamphlets. Her poems have won prizes and been broadcast. She was writer in residence at Gladstone's Library in 2013.

Claire Trévien is the Anglo-Breton author of *Low-Tide Lottery* (Salt, 2011) and *The Shipwrecked House* (Penned in the Margins, 2013), which was longlisted in the Guardian First Book Awards. www.clairetrevien.co.uk

Tim Turnbull started tap dancing lessons when he was 46. A year later, after two separate weeks in bed with his back, he was forced to give up his dream. His poetry, however, is published by Donut Press, which is some consolation.

Deborah Tyler-Bennett's latest collections are a volume of poetry inspired by Keats House where she was a resident writer in 2010, *Kinda Keats* (Shoestring, 2013), and *Turned Out Nice Again* (King's England, 2013) a book of short fictions set in variety during the 1940s.

Ryan Van Winkle is a poet, live artist, podcaster and critic. He is currently Edinburgh City Libraries' Poet-in-Residence. His first collection, *Tomorrow, We Will Live Here*, was published by Salt in 2010. www.ryanvanwinkle.com.

Fiona Ritchie Walker is originally from Montrose, now living in Blaydon. Her poetry has been included in many anthologies and her latest collection, *The Second Week of the Soap*, was published by Red Squirrel Press in 2013.

Max Wallis's pamphlet, *Modern Love*, was shortlisted for the Polari First Book Prize. He graduated from Manchester University with a Distinction in Creative Writing and now lives in London where he works as a model and finishing his debut novel, *Legacies*. www.max-wallis.com.

Tony Walsh, a.k.a. Longfella, is a full-time poet who performs and teaches around the UK. In 2013, he was invited to perform 'The Last Gang In Town?' at a BBC 6 Music recording of An Audience With The Clash at London's famous Maida Vale studios, where the band's Mick Jones asked for a signed copy.

Richard Watt writes for a morning newspaper in Scotland. He divides his time between being a proud father, sitting in courtrooms and being shouted at by farmers. His pamphlet *The Golem* was published by Holdfire in 2012.

Tim Wells: Jason King, the Sweeney, Planet of the Apes, Kung Fu films, reggae music, pie and mash, the Flashing Blade, Ingrid Pitt.

Brian Whittingham is a Glasgow author and editor of poetry, short fiction and drama. He lectures in Creative Writing at City of Glasgow College & Kelvingrove Art Gallery. His most recent poetry collection, *Clocking In Clocking Out,* was published by Luath Press.

Susan Wicks is a poet, novelist and translator. Her sixth collection, *House of Tongues* (Bloodaxe), was a Poetry Book Society Recommendation. Her second book-length translation of Valerie Rouzeau, *Talking Vrouz,* won the 2014 Oxford-Weidenfeld Prize.

Chrissy Williams is a writer and freelance editor living in London. She is director of the Poetry Book Fair. She has published four pamphlets. *Flying into the Bear* (HappenStance, 2013) was shortlisted for the Michael Marks Awards.

Colin Will is an Edinburgh-born poet with a background in science. Seven collections published, the latest being *The Propriety of Weeding,* from Red Squirrel Press (2012). A collection of haibun, *The Book of Ways,* is due from Red Squirrel in October 2014. He chairs the Board of the StAnza poetry festival.

Tony Williams has published two collections of poetry, *The Corner of Arundel Lane and Charles Street* and *The Midlands,* and *All the Rooms of Uncle's Head,* a pamphlet of sonnets. He also writes prose fiction.

Andrew J. Wilson's stories, poems and essays have been published all over the world, sometimes in very unlikely places. With Neil Williamson, he co-edited *Nova Scotia: New Scottish Speculative Fiction.*

Naomi Woddis is a writer, photographer and radio presenter. She created the Poetry Mosaic, an innovative online collaboration with an international following. She was Writer in Residence at Culpeper Community Garden, Islington and also hosted the radio show 'The Conversational' on Reel Rebels Radio.

Dawn Wood grew up in Omagh, Co. Tyrone, and now lives in Perthshire, where she works as a hypnotherapist. Her poetry publications include *Quarry* and *Ingathering* (Templar poetry, 2008, 2013).

Rodney Wood is retired and lives in Farnborough. His poetry has recently appeared in *Screech Owl, The Lake, Stride* and *Prole* magazines, and he was shortlisted for the 2014 Poetry School/ Pighog Prize.

Luke Wright is an Essex boy made good, he now lives in Suffolk. His debut collection is *Mondeo Man* (Penned in the Margins). He likes a bit of *Abba*.